Self-Working
Rope Magic
70 Foolproof Tricks

by Karl Fulves

With 423 Illustrations by
Joseph K. Schmidt

DOVER PUBLICATIONS, INC.
New York

Copyright © 1990 by Karl Fulves.
All rights reserved under Pan American and International
Copyright Conventions.

Published in Canada by General Publishing Company, Ltd.,
30 Lesmill Road, Don Mills, Toronto, Ontario.
Published in the United Kingdom by Constable and Company,
Ltd., 3 The Lanchesters, 162–164 Fulham Palace Road, London
W6 9ER.

Self-Working Rope Magic: 70 Foolproof Tricks is a new work,
first published by Dover Publications, Inc., in 1990.

Manufactured in the United States of America
Dover Publications, Inc., 31 East 2nd Street, Mineola, N.Y.
11501

Library of Congress Cataloging-in-Publication Data

Fulves, Karl.
    Self-working rope magic : 70 foolproof tricks / by Karl
Fulves ; with 423 illustrations by Joseph K. Schmidt.
        p.   cm.
    ISBN 0-486-26541-2
    1. Tricks.   2. Conjuring.   3. Rope.   4. Knots and splices.
I. Schmidt, Joseph K.   II. Title.
GV1559.F85   1990
793.8—dc20   90-47958
                                                            CIP

Foreword

Rope magic is one of the oldest branches of magic. It is also one of the most modern. The basic apparatus has not changed in the four centuries since a rope trick was described in Reginald Scot's *Discoverie of Witchcraft* (1584). Perhaps because of the absolute simplicity of the apparatus, rope tricks have always enjoyed a streamlined, up-to-the-minute appearance.

Rope magic may be the ideal way for beginners to become acquainted with the basic principles of magic. The apparatus is inexpensive, there are no special gimmicks and no palming or other difficult sleights are called for. On the other hand, rope tricks require just enough handling to make them challenging to the beginner.

Generally, rope tricks are grouped into broad categories (knots, cut and restored, penetrations, etc.). The tricks in this book are arranged differently. The book consists of 11 short chapters, each dealing with a particular specialty. The reader who wishes to put together a rope act can thus pick a trick from each of several chapters and be assured of having varied effects and methods.

In this century, rope magic has been popularized by Harlan Tarbell, Milbourne Christopher, Stewart James and R. C. Buff. The reader wishing further rope material should consult the book compiled by James, *Abbott's Encyclopedia of Rope Tricks for Magicians* (Dover 0-486-23206-9).

For their assistance in compiling the material in this book I would like to thank Howard Wurst, Sam Schwartz, Louis Tannen, Inc., Martin Gardner and Joseph K. Schmidt.

KARL FULVES

Contents

Special Effects   47

Flourish Knots   54

Dissolving Knots   65

Cut-and-Restored Rope   77

The Hunter Knot   99

Ropes That Think   107

Miracle Move   123

Psychic Rope Ties   130

The Preliminaries

Use soft, untreated white cotton clothesline for the tricks in this book. A supply of inexpensive rope can be found in department and hardware stores. Cut off the length you want. Then remove the core by pulling it from the outer sleeve as shown in Figure 1. Discard the core. When the rope has been cored you will find that it is soft and flexible.

To keep the ends from fraying with use, they can be taped as shown in Figure 2. You can also dip the ends of the rope into a clear adhesive and let them dry. A method favored by some professional magicians is to wind white thread around the ends. A simple alternative is to trim the ends of the rope before using it.

Fig. 1   **Fig. 2**

For many of the tricks in this book a rope about 36″ long is recommended. Experiment with different lengths. Pick the one you feel comfortable with. If a longer rope is required, a good rule of thumb is to measure off a piece that goes from the outstretched hand to the foot as shown in Figure 3.

When performing knot-tying tricks, you may find that a kink or twist develops in the rope. A quick way to remove the twist is to run the hand over the rope several times as shown in Figure 4.

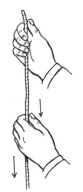

Fig. 3   **Fig. 4**

Sometimes a trick gains in effect if a rope of a color other than white is used. The easiest way to obtain such rope is to purchase it through a magic shop. Sashcord is a good substitute. It can be obtained in specialty shops. Colored ribbon can be substituted for rope in some tricks in this book.

Some of the tricks require rings. Large plastic rings may be found in ring-toss games. Smaller plastic and wooden bracelets are obtainable in department stores. Brass rings up to 3″ in diameter are sold in leather-goods shops. Wooden rings in a variety of sizes can be found in shops stocking embroidery goods. If you do not have a ready supply of rings, you can still try out most of the ring tricks in this book with rings cut from cardboard. The flat kind shown in Figure 5 can be cut from cardboard. The kind shown in Figure 6 can be cut from circular cardboard boxes like oatmeal boxes.

Fig. 5   Fig. 6

Sometimes a rope must be prepared in advance. Typical is the trick in which a rope has been knotted beforehand. The knots must be concealed from audience view when the trick is introduced. The prepared rope can be placed on the table behind some other object. It can also be kept in a briefcase from which apparatus is removed as required in the performance. Still another approach is to keep the rope in the inside pocket as shown in Figure 7. The right hand opens the jacket. The left hand reaches inside and grasps the rope in such a way as to conceal the knot in the closed fingers.

Rope tricks lend themselves to many patter possibilities. Circus clowns will use rope as a belt or suspenders. A piece of rope can be substituted for the wire that connects the phone to the base as shown in Figure 8. Use a toy phone in your act. Mention that a friend taught you a trick over the phone. As you speak, remove the wire (really a piece of rope) and perform a rope trick with it. A piece of rope can also be used to wrap up a box of tricks. Remove the rope, do a trick with it, then do tricks with the other apparatus inside the box.

In some of the tricks in this book the ends of the rope will be labeled with letters of the alphabet. This is to make it clear how the rope is to be handled. You can mark the rope in a similar way so that you have easy visual cues to follow as you learn the handling.

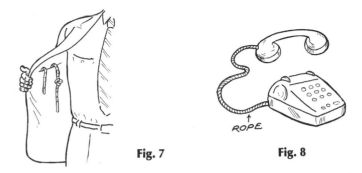

Fig. 7   Fig. 8

Although all of the tricks in this book use rope, some of them can be performed with no loss of effect if string is substituted. The core removed from the rope in Figure 1 contains several strands of soft, flexible cotton string which may be used in such tricks. The advantage gained is that string takes up even less space than rope. If you carry close-up tricks in the pocket and space is a problem, use string instead of rope.

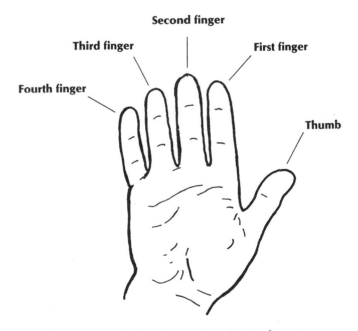

Fingers of the hand, as referred to in the text

The Overhand Knot

Each of these next five chapters is devoted to a particular rope knot. Many of these basic techniques and tricks are used by professional magicians in close-up and platform work.

1. The Basic Overhand Knot

The overhand knot is probably the first knot children learn. For that reason, when you perform magic tricks with overhand knots, even young children can appreciate the magical behavior of the overhand knots you tie. More on the subject, such as one-hand knots and dissolving overhand knots, can be found in subsequent chapters.

To form the knot, hold the rope as in Figure 9, an end in each hand. Cross end A over end B. This produces the situation of Figure 10.

Thread end A through the loop in the direction of the arrow in Figure 10. The result is the overhand knot shown in Figure 11. The overhand knot is sometimes called a half hitch or over-and-under knot.

Youngsters are not aware that it is impossible to tie or untie an overhand knot without letting go of the ends. You can set up a simple challenge by tying the overhand knot of Figure 11. Then ask the child to untie the knot while you hold firmly to the ends of the rope. When he gives up, you can cause the knot to vanish by the following method.

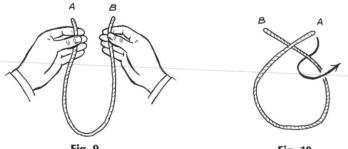

Fig. 9   Fig. 10

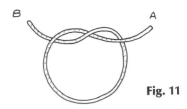

Fig. 11

2. Slide Off

The magician ties an overhand knot in a piece of rope. By simply passing the hand over the knot he causes it to vanish.

Method: Use a piece of rope about 36″ in length. Tie an overhand knot by the method shown in Figures 9–11. As you pull the knot snug, secretly slip the left third finger into the loop, Figure 12. The left hand is closed in a loose fist. The back of the left hand is toward the audience, so the audience cannot see you slip the left third finger into the knot.

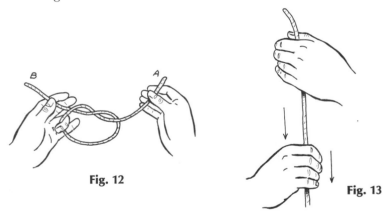

Fig. 12

Fig. 13

Bring the hands to the position shown in Figure 13, the right hand below the left hand. Then pull the rope straight downward with the right hand. As the rope slides through the left hand the knot will be pulled until it dissolves off the end of the rope. This action is concealed because the back of the left hand is toward the audience. From the audience's point of view the knot has simply vanished from the rope.

To finish the trick, when the rope has been pulled completely through the left hand, make a tossing motion with the left hand as if tossing the knot away. Then open the left hand to show it empty. The knot has vanished.

For the stunt to work, do not pull the knot too snug when forming it. If the knot is fairly loose, it will slide smoothly through the left hand.

3. Betcha Knot

The magician demonstrates a simple method of tying a knot in the center of a piece of rope. After he does it several times, he asks the spectator to tie a knot the same way. The spectator is surprised to discover that despite his best efforts he cannot tie a knot in the rope.

Method: The rope can be 18″ to 36″ in length. A piece of string or a shoelace can be substituted for rope.

The starting position is important. One end is clipped between the left first and second fingers so that the end is toward the palm. The other end is clipped between the right first and second fingers so that the end is away from the palm. The starting position is indicated in Figure 14, but this would give away too much information to the spectator, so the actual grip is concealed in the following way.

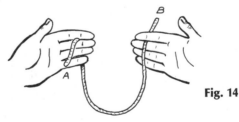

Fig. 14

The left thumb pushes up on end *A*. The right thumb rests against the rope near the point where the rope is clipped between the fingers. The position is shown in Figure 15. It appears as if both hands hold the rope the same way. Anyone who tries to duplicate the feat by gripping the rope the same way with each hand will find it nearly impossible to tie a knot.

Bring the hands together. As you do, separate the first and second fingers from the third and fourth fingers of each hand as shown in Figure 16. At the same time move the left thumb out of the way so end *A* falls as shown in Figure 16.

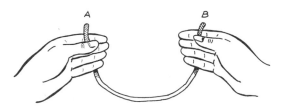

Fig. 15

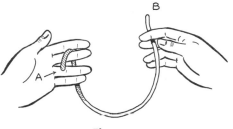

Fig. 16

When the hands are together, clip end *A* between the right second and third fingers. Simultaneously clip end *B* between the left second and third fingers as shown in Figure 17.

Move the hands apart and the knot of Figure 18 will form in the rope. Drop the rope on the table. Ask the spectator to duplicate the feat. Even if you demonstrate the method two or three times he should find it impossible to tie a knot in the rope.

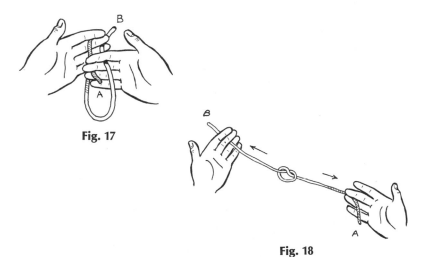

Fig. 17

Fig. 18

4.   Triple Knots

Based on a clever trick of Milbourne Christopher's, this is a fine opening trick. As the audience sees it, the magician shows a piece of rope and separates his hands. Three genuine knots instantly appear on the rope.

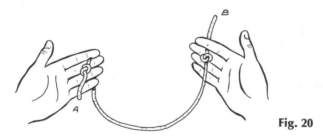

Fig. 19

Method: The handling is the same as the Betcha Knot (No. 3) but there is some preparation. Before you do the trick, tie a knot in the rope near each end, Figure 19. The position depends on the length you use. If you use an 18″ piece of rope, the knots should be about 3″ from the ends. If you plan to do other rope tricks and require a longer rope, use a 36″ length and make the knots 6″ from the ends. The knots should not be drawn too snug.

Fig. 20

The trick is done as an opening trick. Hold the rope as shown in Figure 20. This grip is the same as in Figure 14 of the Betcha Knot, but the extra knots are concealed in the hands. The backs of the hands are toward the audience.

Form the Betcha Knot as shown in Figures 16–18. The result will be three knots in the rope as shown in Figure 21. The appearance of three knots is surprising and a signal for applause from the audience.

Fig. 21

5.   Dissolving Double Knot

Two ropes are tied together with a double overhand knot. The spectator pulls the knot as tight as he wishes, yet the ropes immediately separate from one another.

Method: The ropes are about 18″ long. For clarity one rope will be shown shaded in the diagrams.

Hold one rope in each hand near the end. Cross the end of the left hand's rope over the right hand's rope, Figure 22. With the aid of the thumbs and first fingers, twist end *B* around end *A* so that they are in the position shown in Figure 23. As you do this, remark that you will tie the ropes together securely with a double knot. The twist of Figure 23 appears to be the first knot.

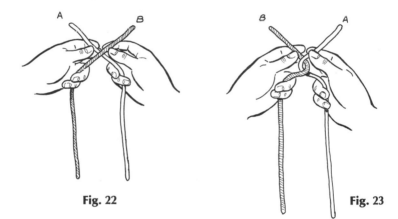

Fig. 22   Fig. 23

Cross end *B* over on top of end *A*. Hold end *B* in place with the right thumb and first finger. The position is shown in Figure 24. Then bring end *A* around end *B* in the direction shown by the

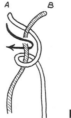

Fig. 24

arrow in Figure 24. Pull the knot tight as in Figure 25. The spectator can even tug on the knot to tighten it as long as you hold the knot in place with the thumbs and first fingers.

Grasp both ropes at the knot with the right hand and place them in the left hand, Figure 26. Pretend to adjust the upper and lower ends of the ropes with the right hand. You really allow the strands below the knot to unravel.

Grasp the ropes below the knots as shown in Figure 27. Separate the hands with a quick motion. The ropes will magically separate from one another.

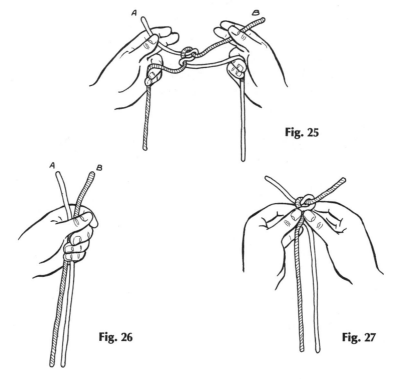

Fig. 25

Fig. 26

Fig. 27

6. The Captive Knot

One of the classic tricks with an overhand knot is to tie a knot in the center of a piece of rope, then knot the ends together. The spectator is asked if he can untie the overhand knot without first untying the ends of the rope. When he gives up, the magician performs the feat by an apparently magical means.

The following is an up-to-date approach to this trick.

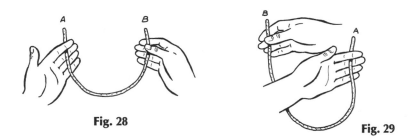

Fig. 28

Fig. 29

Method: Use a rope about 36″ in length. You are seated at the table across from the spectator. Hold the ends of the rope as shown in Figure 28. Bring the right hand behind the left hand as shown in Figure 29. Then bring the rope across the left palm to the position of Figure 30.

Hold end *A* firmly between the left first and second fingers. Using the right hand, tie an overhand knot in the rope with end *B* as shown in Figure 31.

With the rope in the position shown in Figure 31, have the spectator grasp the ends. Slip your hands out of the loops. The spectator ties the ends together with three or four knots. The situation is

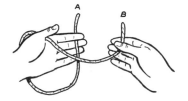

Fig. 30

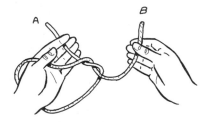

Fig. 31

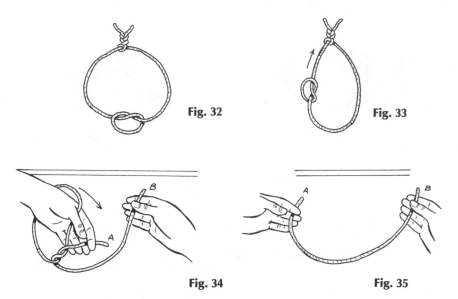

Fig. 32   Fig. 33

Fig. 34   Fig. 35

shown in Figure 32. Ask him if he can untie the overhand knot without untying the ends of the rope.

When he gives up, take the rope from him. Place it below the level of the tabletop. Run the overhand knot up to join the knotted ends of the rope as shown in Figure 33. Tighten the overhand knot so it blends in with the other knots. Then bring the rope up into view. The knot has apparently been untied by magic. Slydini has suggested that after you have brought the overhand knot up to join the other knots, you tie a tangled slip knot in the center of the rope. Then bring the rope up into view. Pull the rope and the knot dissolves. Thus the audience thinks it actually saw you dissolve the overhand knot.

Offer to repeat the trick. Untie the rope. Then form the knot by the method shown in Figures 28–31. But this time, instead of handing the ends of the rope to the spectator, slide the rope off the left wrist and into the lap, Figure 34.

It appears as if you tied a knot in a rope and merely dropped the knotted center of the rope into the lap. In fact, the knot will dissolve as soon as it slides free of the hands, Figure 35. The spectator is unaware of this, since the center of the rope is in the lap and therefore out of his view.

Hand the ends of the rope to the spectator to hold. Keep the center of the rope in the lap. Tangle the center of the rope, then bring it into view. Slowly pull the tangles out to show the knot is gone.

7.   Ghost Knot

The magician demonstrates how to tie a knot in a rope while the spectator holds the ends. The spectator then ties a slip knot in the center of the rope. While he holds the ends, the magician magically converts the slip knot to an overhand knot.

The finish is unexpected. While the ends of the rope are in view, the magician causes the center of the rope to become linked to a buttonhole in his jacket!

Method: This ingenious routine was devised by Horace Bennett. Two ropes are used. One rope is switched for the other but the clever angle is that the rope is switched a little at a time and in full view of the audience.

You need a rope about 48″ in length and a duplicate rope of the same length. Preparation consists in tying a knot near the center of the duplicate rope. This extra rope is secretly put on the lap at the start of the routine. One way to do this is to have each rope coiled in the inside jacket pocket. Remove both together and place them in the lap. Then bring the unprepared rope into view.

The spectator is seated across from you at the table. He may also be seated at the right. Tie a loose knot in the unprepared rope and have the spectator hold the ends of the rope. Explain that you cannot untie the knot unless the spectator lets go of the ends.

Take the ends from him and untie the knot. Now pretend to tie a knot in the center of the rope again, but in fact tie a false knot. To do this hold the rope as shown in Figure 36. Move the right hand forward and to the left, creating a loop in the rope, Figure 37.

Hold the loop between the left thumb and first finger, Figure

Fig. 36   **Fig. 37**

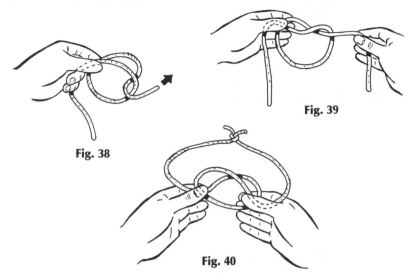

Fig. 39

Fig. 38

Fig. 40

38. Let the right end of the rope fall free in front of the loop. Then thread it through the loop in the direction of the arrow in Figure 38. Display the false knot as shown in Figure 39.

Drop the center of the rope into the lap. Hand the ends of the rope to the spectator and tell him to hold them firmly.

Place the hands below the level of the tabletop. Quickly thread one end of the duplicate rope through your jacket buttonhole, pulling about 6" of rope through.

Now take the center of the other rope and make a jumbled knot of it. Of course this is a fake knot but it should look complicated, as if you tried and apparently failed to untie the knot in the center of the rope by magic.

Bring this false knot up into view and put the center of the rope on the table. Then commence to untie it by pulling out one loop at a time, turning it this way and that, until the knot is completely untied.

Offer to repeat the trick. Again tie the fake knot of Figures 36–39. Drop the center of the rope into the lap. Then take the ends of the rope, tie them and hand them to the spectator.

As you go to the lap to form a complicated fake knot in the center of the rope, pull the end of the duplicate rope a bit further through the buttonhole and tie the ends of the rope together in the same manner as you did the ends of the rope held by the spectator.

Bring the center of the first rope into view, displaying the complicated knot in the center, Figure 40. Untie the knot as described above.

Here the routine changes. Take the knotted ends of the visible rope from the spectator and hand him the center of the rope. Ask him to try to tie a knot in the center of the rope. The patter is to the effect that it is not as easy as it may look.

While he is trying to tie a knot in the center of the rope, drop the hand holding the knotted ends of the rope into the lap. Drop these ends and immediately grasp the knotted ends of the duplicate rope that is threaded through the buttonhole.

Ask the spectator to form a slip knot in the center of the rope. Then take the knotted center of the rope from the spectator and as you bring it to your lap, the hands move in unison. Bring the knotted ends of the duplicate rope into sight and hand them to the spectator. Figure 41 shows the situation at this point. Figure 42 shows the view from the spectator's angle.

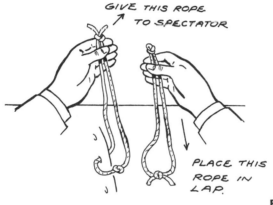

Fig. 41

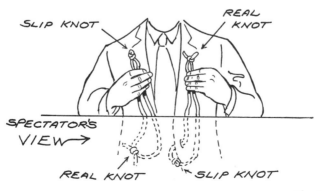

Fig. 42

Note that at this point in the routine you have switched half of the original rope; the ends of the duplicate rope are being handed over to the spectator while the center of the original rope is being dropped into the lap.

The original rope is discarded completely since it is no longer used. You can leave it on the lap at this point.

Tell the spectator you will convert the slip knot he made in the center of the rope into a real knot. With the hands out of sight under the table, loosen the knot in the center of the duplicate rope and pull several loops through it. The idea, once again, is to make a complicated-looking knot in the center of the rope.

Place this knotted section on the table. Since the rope is threaded through the buttonhole of the jacket, it will be necessary for you to sit forward somewhat to conceal the true situation.

Slowly unravel the knotted section in the center of the rope until it is seen that a real knot is left in the rope. This in itself is a strong effect that should lead the spectator to conclude the routine is over.

Start to hand the rope to the spectator with the remark that he may try to untie the knot in the center. It suddenly becomes apparent that the rope itself has somehow become linked to the buttonhole of your jacket, an unexpected and quite remarkable finish to the routine.

The Slip Knot

The slip knot is the easiest trick knot. Youngsters find it to be one of the most magical knots. Form a slip knot in a rope, pull it snug and have a youngster close his fist around the knot. Pull the ends of the rope so that the knot dissolves. The child will open his fist, amazed that the knot has vanished.

This chapter contains a number of tricks with slip knots. It closes with a brilliant routine of Jack Miller's that is ideal for close-up or platform work.

8. Quick Slip Knot

Use a rope about 36" long. Hold the rope in the right hand as shown in Figure 43, so that one strand is between the thumb and first finger, while the other strand is between the second and third fingers. Pull the center of the rope out so it is about 3" from the fingers. With the left hand palm down, slip the left first and second fingers into the loop as shown in Figure 43.

Twist the left hand so it is palm up, Figure 44. Then slide the left first and second fingers through the loop in the direction shown by the arrow in Figure 44 and clip the upper strand. The position is shown in Figure 45.

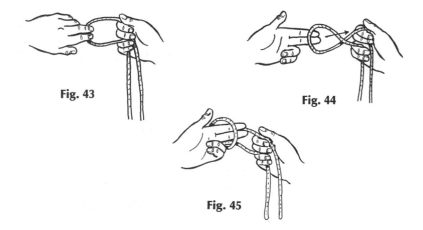

Fig. 43

Fig. 44

Fig. 45

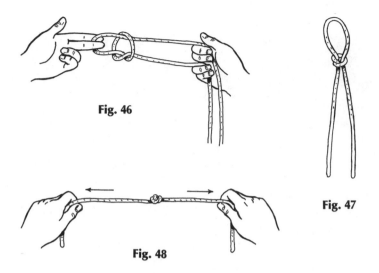

Fig. 46

Fig. 47

Fig. 48

Pull the clipped strand back to the left. At the same time, allow the loop around the left first and second fingers to slide off the fingers. If it does not easily slide off, push it off with the aid of the left thumb. The result is the situation of Figure 46.

You can tighten the knot to form a noose as in Figure 47, or you can pull the loop snug to form a knot as in Figure 48.

There are many ways to form slip knots. This is a quick, easy method that can be done as one continuous motion.

9.   Slippery Knot

The magician forms a slip knot in a piece of rope. While the spectator holds the ends of the rope, the magician performs the impossible feat of converting the slip knot to a genuine overhand knot.

Method: Beforehand, tie an overhand knot in the center of a piece of rope. Conceal this knot in the right palm when you bring the rope forward. The slip knot is formed in a manner similar to the Quick Slip Knot. Hold the rope in the right hand so that one strand is between the thumb and first finger. The other strand is between the second and third fingers. The knot rests under the right thumb. The position is shown in the exposed view of Figure 49. In performance, the hand would be closed in a loose fist to conceal the knot.

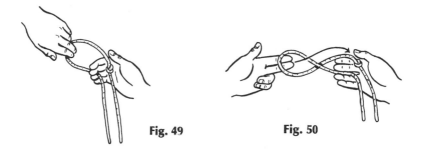

Fig. 49   Fig. 50

With the left hand palm down, slip the left first and second fingers through the loop as shown in Figure 49. Turn the left hand palm up to put a twist in the rope as shown in Figure 50.

The left first and second fingers reach through the loop in the direction shown by the arrow in Figure 50, but instead of grasping the strand, they clip the knot as indicated in Figure 51. Pull the knot through the loop that is around the left first and second fingers. The fingers conceal the knot from audience view.

Allow the loop to slide off the fingers, but do not release your grip on the overhand knot. As far as the audience is concerned, you have simply formed a slip knot in the center of the rope.

Bring the center of the rope to a position below the level of the tabletop. Toss the ends of the rope out onto the table as shown in Figure 52. Remark that you will try to convert the slip knot into a genuine knot without going near the ends of the rope. The spectator can hold the ends of the rope.

Drop the hands to the lap. Loosen the slip knot and pass it over the overhand knot. Then pull the slip knot so it dissolves. Loosen the overhand knot a bit, then bring it into view.

You have performed the impossible feat of converting a false knot to a genuine knot while the spectator held the ends of the rope.

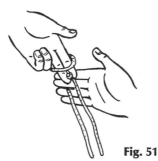

Fig. 51

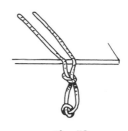

Fig. 52

Fig. 53

Another presentation is to dissolve the slip knot as described above, then form a new slip knot by passing a strand of rope through the overhand knot in the direction shown by the arrow in Figure 53. Bring the center of the rope into view. The spectator pulls on the ends of the rope. The slip knot visibly changes to an overhand knot.

10. Ringo

A borrowed finger ring is threaded onto the center of a piece of rope. The spectator clearly sees his ring being placed on the rope. On command the ring penetrates the table.

Method: In this trick a slip knot is used to form a hook in a piece of rope. The borrowed ring is secretly hooked onto the slip knot and stolen away.

Beforehand, form a slip knot near one end of a 36″ piece of rope. The position of the slip knot will vary depending on individual preference, but typically it will be about 3″ from the end of the rope. Adjust the loop of the slip knot so it extends about ½″ from the knot. Hold the rope in the right hand with the slip knot concealed in the right palm. The spectator should be seated across from you.

Ask to borrow his ring. Hold the ring in the left hand between thumb and first finger. The starting position is shown in Figure 54.

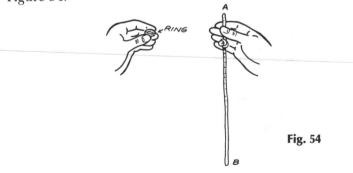

Fig. 54

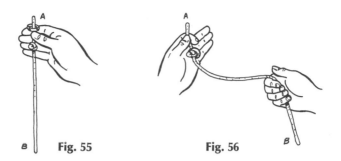

B   **Fig. 55**   **Fig. 56**   B

Drop the ring over the top of the rope, Figure 55. The ring rests on the right thumb and first finger at this point. Allow the spectator to see clearly that the ring has been threaded onto the end of the rope.

Grasp end *A* of the rope with the left thumb and first finger. Allow the ring to slip into the right palm just above the slip knot. The left second, third and fourth fingers should extend straight out. Do not curl them inward because the spectator may suspect that you are trying to palm the ring. Lift end *A* upward. The ring rests on the slip knot and is stolen into the left palm as shown in Figure 56. The back of the left hand faces the spectator, so the ring is concealed from view. Look at the right hand as if it still contained the ring.

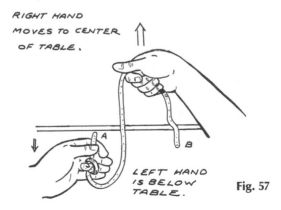

RIGHT HAND MOVES TO CENTER OF TABLE.

LEFT HAND IS BELOW TABLE.   **Fig. 57**

Bring the right hand toward the center of the table. At the same time, drop the left hand to a position below the level of the tabletop, as shown in Figure 57. It is important to keep your gaze directed at the right hand. The spectator will assume the right hand contains the ring.

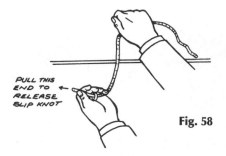

PULL THIS
END TO
RELEASE
SLIP KNOT

Fig. 58

Turn the right hand palm down and place it against the center of the table, Figure 58. The left hand pulls end A of the rope. This causes the slip knot to dissolve, destroying the evidence. Close the left fingers around the ring.

Bring the left hand under the table to a position at the center of the table. Tap the right hand against the tabletop. Release the rope, open the right hand and turn it palm up to show that the ring has vanished. Then bring the left hand into view with the ring.

11.   Name a Number

There is a classic trick in which a spectator names a number, say 4. The magician coils a piece of rope, then tosses the rope into the air, causing four knots to form magically on the rope.

The following is a subtle variation. The magician coils the rope in his hand. The spectator is then asked to name a number between 1 and 4. Whatever number he names, the rope is thrown and that number of knots appears on the rope. The difference between this version and the standard version is that the rope is coiled beforehand. The magician makes no adjustment after the number is named, yet he correctly throws the number of knots named by the spectator.

Method: The presence of a slip knot, unknown to the audience, is what makes the trick easy to do. Use a piece of rope about 5′ long. Beforehand, tie a slip knot about 12″ from one end. Pull the knot snug so it resembles an overhand knot. The prepared rope is shown in Figure 59.

A   B

SLIP KNOT   **Fig. 59**

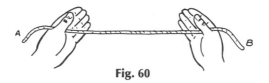

Fig. 60

When demonstrating the trick, hold the rope so that the slip knot is concealed under the left thumb. Both hands are palm up as shown in Figure 60. As you show the rope, ask a spectator to think of a number between 1 and 4.

You are now going to form two throw knots in the rope. The following is based on Harlan Tarbell's description of this standard technique. Slide the right hand along the rope to a point about a third of the way from the left end. Then turn the right hand to the position shown in Figure 61 to form a loop in the rope.

Bring this loop to the left hand. Hold it in place with the left thumb as shown in Figure 62.

Repeat the same process to form a second loop. The situation is shown in Figure 63. Bring end *B* up and clip it between the left second and third fingers as indicated in Figure 64. Ask the spectator for the number he is thinking of. Since you asked for a number *between* 1 and 4, his number can only be 2 or 3.

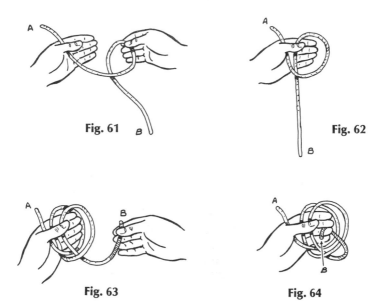

Fig. 61   B

Fig. 62

B

Fig. 63

Fig. 64

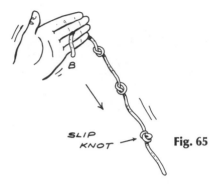

Fig. 65

Hold end *B* firmly as you throw the rope downward. The result is shown in Figure 65. Three knots have appeared on the rope. If the spectator named 3, take your bow.

If he named 2, show the rope as in Figure 65. Pretend to notice your mistake, apologize for throwing too many knots, and pull on the ends of the rope. One knot will vanish, leaving 2 knots on the rope.

Even if the spectator names 3, you can show 3 knots on the rope as in Figure 65, then say, "Many people wonder, suppose they named 2 instead?" Pull on the slip knot with the hands, causing it to dissolve. Say, "One knot would leave."

Make sure the loops formed in Figures 61 and 62 are large. The knots will then form without the rope becoming tangled. It is not too well known that you can throw figure-8 knots into a rope as easily as overhand knots. To try it out, form the loop of Figure 62, then give the loop one more twist in the same direction. Grasp end *B* as in Figure 64. Throw the rope downward. A figure 8 will form in the center of the rope.

12. Convertible Knot

This is an unusual knot which resembles a slip knot but converts into an overhand knot. One version is shown in Figure 53. To form the convertible knot, first tie an overhand knot in a piece of rope. Then form a loop in one strand and pass it through the knot in the direction of the arrow shown in Figure 66.

Fig. 66

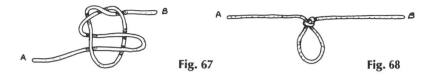

Fig. 67   Fig. 68

The result is shown in Figure 67. Pull the overhand knot tight. You now have a knot that looks like a slip knot, in Figure 68. The noose or loop will even tighten like a slip knot. But at the point where the loop is pulled snug, one more tug on the rope will cause the slip knot to dissolve, leaving you with a genuine overhand knot.

To use the convertible knot in a routine, tie a knot as in Figure 68. The noose should be about an inch in diameter. Conceal this knot in the left palm.

Have a spectator hold the ends of the rope. Remark that you know a simple way to tie a slip knot in the rope while the spectator holds the ends. Grasp the rope as shown in Figure 69.

Form a loop by twisting one strand over the other as shown in Figure 70. Then reach through the loop in the direction of the arrow in Figure 70 with the right first finger and thumb. Grasp the rope at X and pull it through to form the slip knot shown in Figure 71.

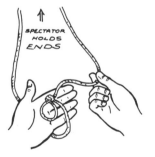

Fig. 69

Fig. 70

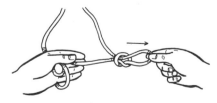

Fig. 71

The spectator will probably be little impressed since he too can tie the same sort of knot. Remark that you will convert the slip knot to a genuine knot while the spectator holds the ends of the rope.

Place the slip knot into the left palm. Pull the rope to the right, Figure 72, causing the slip knot to dissolve while it is in the palm. Then pull the convertible knot into view. It looks as if nothing has changed. Continue pulling on the knot until the knot visibly converts to an overhand knot.

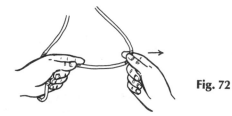

Fig. 72

13.   Soap on a Rope

A bar of soap is used in this novel trick. It has a hole drilled through it. The rope is knotted onto the center of a rope. The magician makes sawing motions with the rope and proceeds to saw through the soap completely. At the finish, both soap and rope are unharmed and may be left with the audience.

Method: Required are a piece of rope about 42″ in length and a short piece measuring about 8″ in length. Also needed is a bar of soap with a hole drilled or carved through it. In this trick a slip knot is used to hold the extra loop in place around the soap.

Preparation is as follows. Tie a slip knot in the center of the long rope as shown in Figure 73. The designations *A, B, C* refer to portions of the rope that will tighten the loop later on.

Thread the short piece through the soap, Figure 74. This piece

Fig. 73   **Fig. 74**

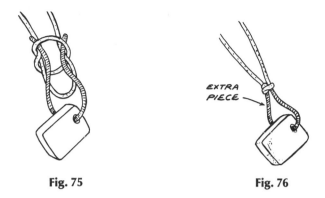

Fig. 75   Fig. 76

of rope is shown shaded so its placement can be clearly followed. Slide the ends of the short piece into the slip knot as in Figure 75.

The slip knot is tightened as follows. Grasp the rope at *A* with the left hand and at *B* with the right hand. Pull *A* upward and B downward. The knot in the slip knot will tighten around the short piece, securing it in place. Then grasp the knot with one hand and *C* with the other hand. Pull *C* upward. The loop in the slip knot will tighten. Continue tightening the knot until the loop is hidden inside the knot. The result will be that the rope looks like Figure 76. The extra piece appears to be the loop in the slip knot.

Display the rope by taking an end in each hand. Swing the rope back and forth. Remark that you are always losing soap in the shower and that you discovered this way to keep track of where it is.

Then lower the rope into the lap. Grasp the soap between the knees and hold it in place. The audience sees the situation of Figure 77. Explain that even though the soap is securely tied to the rope, when the soap is submerged under water, a peculiar thing happens.

With a gentle sawing motion, work the ends of the rope back and forth, slowly tightening the slip knot in the process. The slip knot will dissolve. The extra piece will drop away and the soap will be

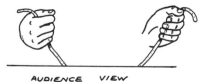

AUDIENCE   VIEW

Fig. 77

free. Separate the hands, causing the full length of the rope to come into view. Then take the soap from between the knees and toss it onto the table. Soap and rope may be left for examination.

The spectator can scratch his initials in the soap at the start of the routine. This does away with the suspicion that the soap is switched. When the routine has been concluded, you can drop the rope into the lap, then pick up the rope plus the extra piece and place them into the pocket.

14. Miller's Sliding Knots

Jack Miller devised a brilliant impromptu routine in which a slip knot slides from one end of the rope to the other. I am indebted to Howard Wurst for the following description.

Method: Use a rope about 42″ long. Stand facing the audience. Hold the rope as shown in Figure 78. Bring end *B* up to a position between the left thumb and first finger. The situation is shown in Figure 79. Note that end *B* crosses over end *A*. Note too that the rope is clipped between the left first and second fingers. Maintain firm pressure at the point where the left first and second fingers clip the rope.

The right hand reaches through the loop in the direction shown by the arrows in Figure 79. The right thumb and first finger grasp end *A* and bring it back through the loop. At the same time the left hand turns so it is palm toward the audience as shown in Figure

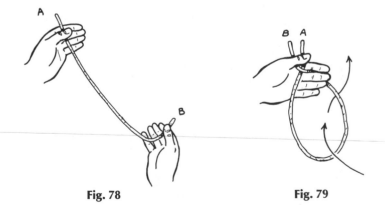

Fig. 78   **Fig. 79**

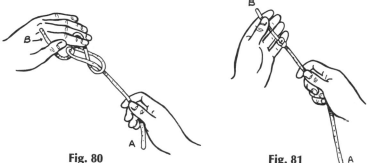

Fig. 80   Fig. 81

Fig. 82

80. The rope is still firmly clipped between the left first and second fingers.

Pull the knot tight. Then release the portion clipped between the left first and second fingers. This portion is the loop of the slip knot. Pull the lower part of the rope with the right hand so that the loop tightens. There is now a slip knot tied near end *B* of the rope, as shown in Figure 81.

It is important that the slip knot be positioned so that when the left fingers curl inward, the slip knot will be concealed in the left palm. Check that the slip knot is correctly positioned. If not, work it upward with the left thumb and first finger until it is properly positioned.

Remark that a slip knot is so named because it can slip. As you say this, close the right hand around the knot as shown in Figure 82. Draw the right hand down the rope as if pulling the slip knot

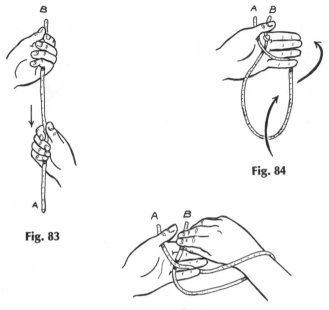

Fig. 84

Fig. 83

Fig. 85

downward. In fact, you simply slide the right hand down the rope. As the right hand moves past the left hand, close the left fingers around the slip knot to conceal it from audience view, Figure 83.

The above sequence requires a bit of acting to make it seem genuine. Act as if a certain amount of strength is required to pull the knot downward. When the right hand has slid completely off the lower end of the rope, pantomime throwing the knot onto the floor, watching it bounce into the air and catching it with the right hand. Then pantomime putting it into your right trouser pocket.

You are now going to repeat the trick. Although it will look like the same effect to the audience, you are one ahead of them because there is a slip knot concealed in the left palm.

Turn slightly so the back of the left hand is toward the audience. Take end A with the right hand and place it between the left thumb and first finger as shown in Figure 84. It is important that the rope be clipped between the left third and fourth fingers.

Reach through the loop with the right hand in the direction of the arrows shown in Figure 84. Grasp end B at the knot as shown in Figure 85 with the right first and second fingers on top, the thumb below. Draw end B through the loop but retain the right hand's grip on the concealed slip knot.

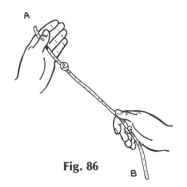

Fig. 86

When forming the second slip knot, remember to turn the left hand so the palm is outward as in Figure 80. Remember too, that the left third and fourth fingers must retain their grip on the rope in order for the slip knot to form. Once the slip knot has been made, release the grip of the left third and fourth fingers. Then pull the loop snug.

As the rope is drawn taut, a slip knot will form near end *A*. The audience is unaware that there is another slip knot near the lower end of the rope, concealed by the right thumb and fingers. The situation is shown in Figure 86.

Make sure the upper knot is in a position where it will be concealed when the left fingers are closed around it. Reach up with the right hand as shown in Figure 87, still keeping the knot in that hand concealed from audience view. Close the right hand around the upper knot and pretend to slide it down the rope.

Continue sliding the right hand down the rope until the lower slip knot is about to slide into view. Then release the right hand

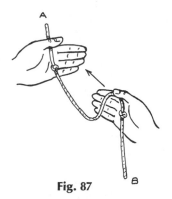

Fig. 87

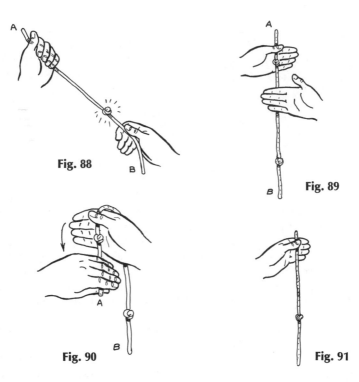

Fig. 88

Fig. 89

Fig. 90

Fig. 91

and grasp the rope below the slip knot to display it as in Figure 88. Note that the closed left hand conceals the other slip knot. The appearance is that you have slid the knot down the rope.

You are now going to exchange the ends of rope as follows. Release the right hand's grip on the rope. Turn the right hand palm up and place it against the rope just below the upper knot as shown in Figure 89. Place the upper slip knot into the right palm, but be careful to keep it concealed from the audience. The left hand simply turns palm down as shown in Figure 90 to deposit the upper knot into the right hand. The back of the right hand is toward the audience, so the knot in the right hand is concealed.

Release the left hand's grip on the rope. Then grasp end *B* with the left hand and raise the left hand to a point above the right hand. The position now is similar to that shown in Figure 86.

Raise the right hand as shown in Figure 87. Close the right hand around the upper knot and pull downward. This time, pull firmly so that the upper knot dissolves. Slide the right hand down the rope until the lower knot comes into view. Display the knot. Once again the knot has magically slid down the rope.

Turn the right hand palm up just under the left hand as in Figure 89. Place the left hand's end of the rope into the right hand. Then grasp the opposite end of the rope with the left hand. The situation after you have changed ends is shown in Figure 91. The audience clearly sees just one knot in the rope.

Grasp the knot with the right hand and pull firmly downward so that the slip knot dissolves. Pantomime sliding the knot off the rope, bouncing it to the floor, catching it and placing it into the pocket. This ends the routine, but if you have two loose knots in the pocket you can toss them out to the spectators for souvenirs.

The Square Knot

The square knot has the unique feature that no matter how firmly the ends of the rope are pulled, the knot only grows tighter. Despite this, magicians have devised ingenious ways to upset the square knot secretly and convert it to a slip knot.

15. Basic Square Knot

The square knot is made from two overhand knots. One way to remember how to tie the square knot is to recall right over left, left over right. Use a 36″ piece of rope. Hold one end in each hand. First cross right over left, that is, the right end over the left end. This is shown in Figure 92.

Thread end A through the loop in the direction shown by the arrow in Figure 92. You are now at the position shown in Figure 93.

Cross left over right. This means that you cross the left end over the right end. The situation is shown in Figure 94. Thread end A through the loop as shown by the arrow in Figure 94. The result is

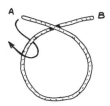

Fig. 92

Fig. 93

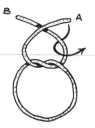

Fig. 94

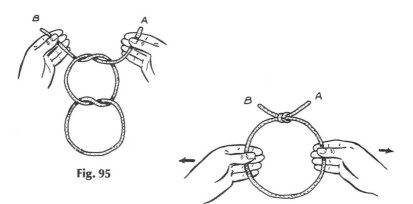

Fig. 95

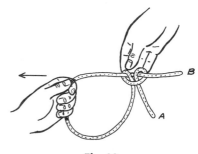

Fig. 96

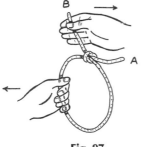

Fig. 97

Fig. 98

the square knot of Figure 95. The square knot is characterized by the fact that the ends are parallel to the strands.

If you grasp the ends as in Figure 95 and pull them apart, the knot will tighten, giving you the snug knot of Figure 96. If more force is applied to the ends, the knot will tighten more. If the strands are grasped as shown in Figure 96, and the hands pulled in opposite directions, the knot will tighten further. This is the feature of the square knot: By pulling the ends or the strands in opposite directions, the knot will only tighten.

There is, however, a simple way to upset the square knot and convert it to a slip knot. Grasp the left strand with one hand and the left end with the other as shown in Figure 97. Pull in opposite directions as indicated by the arrows in Figure 97, and the square knot will convert to the slip knot of Figure 98.

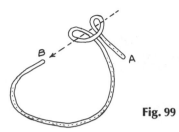

Fig. 99

Grasp the knot with the right hand to hold it in place. Pull the strand with the left hand in the direction of the arrow shown in Figure 98 and the knot will pull free. At the finish the rope will appear as in Figure 99.

16.   The Granny Knot

The granny knot is similar to the square knot in that it is made from two overhand knots. A way to remember how to make the granny knot is to recall the sequence right over left, right over left. For this example use two 36″ pieces of rope. Hold one in each hand. First cross right over left, that is, the right end over the left end as shown in Figure 100. One rope is shown shaded so that the handling will be easier to follow.

Thread end *A* around end *B* in the direction of the arrow shown in Figure 100. The resulting overhand knot is shown in Figure 101.

Cross right over left again. This is shown in Figure 101 with end *B* over end *A*. Then thread end *B* around end *A* as indicated by the arrow in Figure 101. The result is the granny knot of Figure 102. Pull the knot snug.

Note that in Figure 103 the ends are at right angles to the

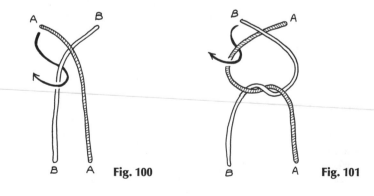

Fig. 100   **Fig. 101**

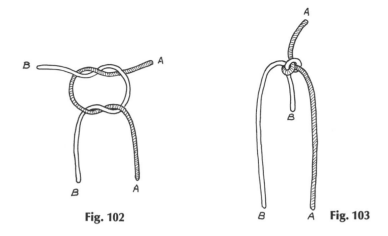

Fig. 102   B   A   **Fig. 103**

strands. This is an easy visual way to tell the difference between a square knot and a granny knot. In a square knot the ends are parallel to the strands; in a granny knot the ends are at right angles to the strands.

If the upper ends of the granny knot are pulled apart, the knot will tighten. If the lower ends are pulled in opposite directions, the knot will also tighten.

To upset the granny knot, grasp the ends of the same rope. Pull them in the direction of the arrows shown in Figure 104 and the knot will convert to a slip knot. The shaded strand can then be slid free of the other strand.

If ropes of the same color are used, you want to be sure you are pulling opposite ends of the same rope. A simple way to do this is to put a pencil dot on each end of one rope. Then you will be sure to grasp the rope properly to convert the granny knot to a slip knot.

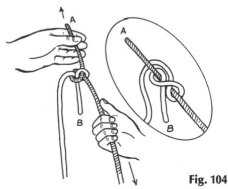

Fig. 104

17. Time in a Knot

The spectator's wristwatch is securely tied to a piece of rope. The spectator himself may tighten the knots. The magician places the rope behind his back. Even though the ends of the rope are tightly knotted, the magician quickly releases the watch.

Method: Use a watch, a solid bracelet or a finger ring—in other words, any circular piece of jewelry that cannot be opened with a clasp. Remark that Houdini used to practice freeing himself from restraints by studying methods like these. As you speak, thread the watch onto the center of the rope. Knot the ends by tying a square knot or a granny knot. Have the spectator tighten the knot by pulling on the ends of the rope.

Put the apparatus behind the back. As soon as the rope is out of sight, upset the knot, converting it to a slip knot. Remove the watch and slip it onto the wrist. Bunch up the rope and hold it in the hand.

Bring the rope out from behind the back. Say, "I give up," as if you could not get the watch free. Put the bunched-up rope into your pocket.

When the spectator objects that his watch is still on the rope, say, "Here, you can have mine." Remove his watch from your wrist and hand it back to him.

18. Half a Square

The magician openly ties a square knot in a piece of rope. The ends of the rope are then tied together by a spectator, Figure 105. The ends may be tied with any number of knots. The ends can also be sealed with adhesive tape.

The magician places the rope out of sight below the tabletop for a moment. When the rope is again brought into view, an overhand knot is seen to have appeared on the rope as shown in Figure 106. The knot is genuine. The ends of the rope have not been tampered with.

Only one piece of rope is used. There are no gimmicks.

Method: After you have tied the square knot in the center of the rope, have the ends tied together by the spectator. He can seal the knotted ends with adhesive tape, then initial the tape to destroy any suspicion that you simply switch ropes.

Place the rope on the lap so it is out of the spectator's view. Loosen the square knot as shown in Figure 107. Bring the lower overhand knot down to the bottom of the rope by tightening this knot.

Then thread the ends of the rope through the upper overhand knot in the direction of the arrow shown in Figure 107. Tighten the knot in the center of the rope. This will form a pseudo-square knot. The appearance is as indicated in Figure 106. It seems as if an overhand knot has appeared in the bottom of the rope.

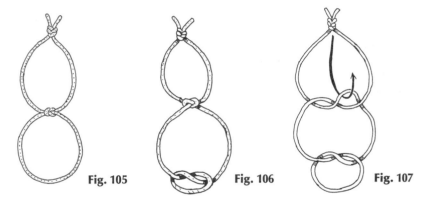

Fig. 105   Fig. 106   Fig. 107

19.   Enough Rope

While traveling in the Orient, a magician was invited to visit the palace of the emperor. At the palace waiting room he chanced to see a golden rope on which were tied two silver rings as shown in Figure 108.

A palace guard explained that anyone who could release the two rings without untying the rope would win the hand of the emperor's beautiful daughter.

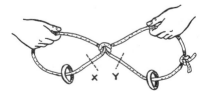

Fig. 108

The magician thought it an easy challenge. He simply cut the rope in two places (shown as X and Y in Figure 108) and removed the silver rings.

"Notify the emperor," he said. "I've released the rings without untying the ropes."

At that point the palace guard remembered another condition; whoever cut the rope would be put to death. The magician's dilemma was clear; how could he restore a rope that had been twice cut at its center?

Method: The rope should be at least 36" in length. Two borrowed finger rings may be used. The other item is an extra knot. This is made by tying a tight knot at one end of the rope. Cut it off the rope. Place the knot in the left jacket pocket.

To perform the trick, display the rope and bring the ends together. Drop one of the rings onto the center of the rope.

Tie a square knot in the center of the rope as shown in Figure 109. Pull the knot snug. Then drop the other ring over one end of the rope. Knot the ends of the rope together.

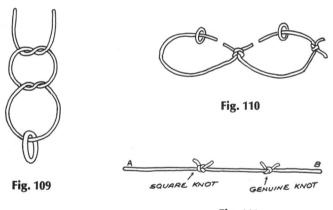

Fig. 110

Fig. 109

SQUARE KNOT   GENUINE KNOT

A   B

Fig. 111

Display the rope as shown in Figure 108. Patter to the effect that the magician's problem was to remove the rings without untying the rope. Take a pair of scissors and cut the rope as shown in Figure 110. Remove the rings.

Remark that the other condition was that the rings were to be removed without cutting the rope. At this point display the rope as in Figure 111. Tug on the ends. This will convert the square knot to a slip knot.

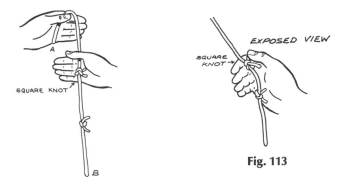

Fig. 113

Fig. 112

Fig. 114

Place the scissors into the left jacket pocket. Grasp the extra knot placed in the pocket earlier. Hold it concealed under the left thumb as that hand is brought out of the pocket.

Place end *A* of the rope into the left hand as shown in Figure 112. Gather the rope into the left hand, accordion-pleating it as you do so.

Note that in Figure 112 the right hand is directly over the square knot. This is an exposed view. In performance, curl the right fingers over the knot as you gather the rope into the left hand. The result will be that the knot slides down the rope, concealed by the right hand, until you reach the position shown in Figure 113. At this point the genuine knot has just entered the right palm.

Pause, tug on the rope, then slowly pull the rope from the left hand. When all of the rope has been pulled free, open the left hand, showing the loose knot. Say, "That's one," and toss the knot onto the table or floor.

The left thumb and first finger now grasp the knot that lies just above the right first finger. Slide this knot off the left end of the rope and toss the knot to the table. Say, "That's two."

Display the rope, apparently restored, between the hands as shown in Figure 114. Unknown to the audience, the right hand conceals the genuine knot in the rope. Gather the rope into the right hand and place it in the pocket.

20.   Siberian Rope Release

One of the best tricks using square knots is a fine routine invented by Eddie Joseph. As the story is told, prisoners carted away to Siberia are tied with three loops of one rope. The first loop is for the neck, the other two for the hands. The magician illustrates the tie by knotting three loops in a piece of rope as shown in Figures 115–120.

If a prisoner tries to escape by cutting the rope, the cut rope will sooner or later be found and other prisoners will be punished as a consequence. One prisoner was a magician. After being bound, he cut all three loops and escaped. The guards never suspected because before he left, the magician restored the rope to one piece.

Method: Required is a 7′ length of rope and a pair of scissors. Place the rope about the neck as in Figure 115. Cross the right strand over the left, Figure 116. Then loop this end through in the direction of the arrow in Figure 116 to form the first knot overhand as shown in Figure 117.

Fig. 115

Fig. 116

Now cross the left strand over the right as in Figure 118. Then loop this end through in the direction of the arrow in Figure 118. Pull the knot snug, Figure 119, but make sure there is slack in the

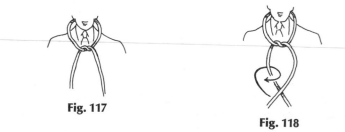

Fig. 117

Fig. 118

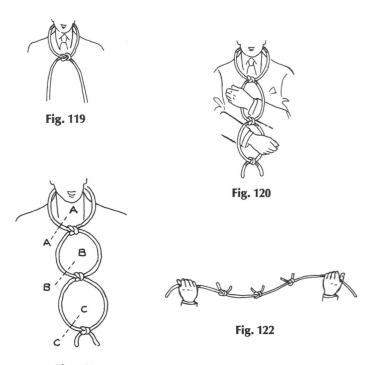

Fig. 119

Fig. 120

Fig. 121

Fig. 122

loop around the neck so you can easily slip the loop over the neck. The above procedure produces a square knot in the rope.

Use the same procedure to form two more square knots at intervals so that two more large loops are formed in the rope. Each time begin by crossing the right strand over the left to make the first knot, then the left strand over the right to make the second knot. The result will be three loops as shown in Figure 120.

Slip the hands through the loops to show how prisoners were transported to Siberia. Then make three cuts with a pair of scissors. Each cut is made just above a square knot. The cuts are shown by *A–A*, *B–B* and *C–C* in Figure 121. Patter that this is how a magician escaped from the rope.

Display the cut rope as shown in Figure 122. All that remains is to slide the knots off the rope to show the rope restored. Remark that one of the other prisoners then used the rope for a belt and no one was ever the wiser.

21.   Square-Knot Paradox

It is an axiom in performing magic that a trick should not be repeated, but in some cases the effect is strengthened by repetition. This square-knot routine, devised by Milbourne Christopher, is an outstanding example. The magician ties the ends of a rope together with a square knot. Although a square knot is supposed to hold up no matter how much strain is put on it, the knot magically dissolves.

The trick is repeated. The audience watches more closely, but once again the square knot magically dissolves. The trick is then done a final time. Although the square knot is slowly and legitimately made, as soon as the magician pulls on it, the knot dissolves.

The strength of this routine lies in the fact that the method is different each time, even though it appears the same to the audience.

Method: The first knot you tie is a square knot, but the second is a knot called a thief knot. Although outwardly it resembles a square knot, it can be dissolved simply by pulling the strands of rope apart. For the sake of simplicity, both knots will be tied by a method different from those described earlier.

For the first phase of the routine, you will tie a genuine square knot in the rope. Begin by forming a loop as shown in Figure 123. Hold the rope in the left hand as in Figure 124 so that end *A* is concealed by the left thumb and first finger.

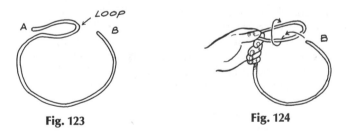

Fig. 123   Fig. 124

Thread end *B* through the loop as shown by the arrows in Figure 124. The situation to this point is shown in Figure 125. Then bring end *B* through the loop in the direction of the arrow in Figure 125 to finish tying the square knot. The result is indicated in Figure 126. Pull the knot almost snug.

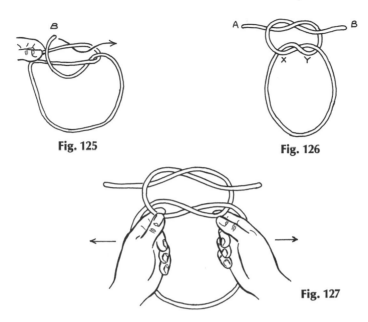

Fig. 125

Fig. 126

Fig. 127

To release the knot, grasp the rope at the point marked X in Figure 126 with the left thumb and first finger. Grasp the point marked Y with the right thumb and first finger.

Pull the hands apart in the directions shown by the arrows in Figure 127. The result is that the square knot will dissolve.

The audience will see that you pulled the knot apart in an unorthodox way, or, if you do it quickly, they may suspect sleight of hand. Offer to repeat the trick. The knot is tied by the same procedure but this time the loop in the left hand has its end below the loop rather than above, as shown in Figure 128. This, of course, is concealed inside the left hand.

The knot is tied by the same procedure as before, as shown by the arrows in Figure 128, but, because the loop was formed differently, the result is the thief knot shown in Figure 129.

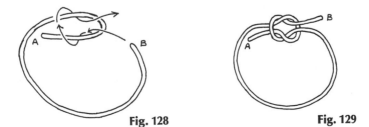

Fig. 128

Fig. 129

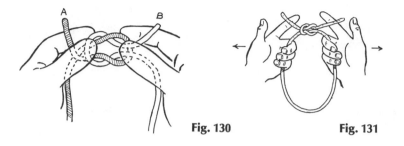

Fig. 130   **Fig. 131**

If you allow the end of the rope in the left hand to cross up and over the long strand, the knot can be displayed as in Figure 130. The crossing is concealed inside the left hand, so the knot appears to be a normal square knot, just as it was displayed before. Do not pull the knot snug, but allow it to remain open, as shown.

Release the pressure of your thumbs and first fingers. Pull the strands outward, in the direction of the arrows shown in Figure 131, and the knot will mysteriously dissolve.

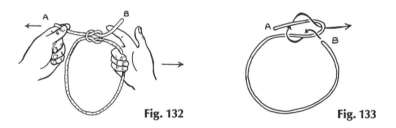

Fig. 132   **Fig. 133**

The audience will be watching very closely when you offer to repeat the trick one more time. That is all to the good because now you will tie a genuine square knot and legitimately cause it to dissolve.

Slowly tie a square knot by the method shown in Figures 123–125. Let the knot remain open. Then grip end A with the left thumb and first finger. Grip the right-hand strand with the right second, third and fourth fingers as shown in the exposed view of Figure 132. The right thumb and first finger would be in contact with end B in actual performance, as if they gripped end B securely, but only light pressure is maintained on end B.

Pull the hands apart in the direction shown by the arrows in Figure 132 and the square knot will dissolve.

If you want to tie a granny knot by the above approach, the method is shown in Figure 133.

Special Effects

There are a number of special knots in rope magic used to create effects of strong visual impact. Some are impromptu and can be set up as part of the trick itself. Some require prior preparation. In each case, the special knot generates a surprising visual effect. This chapter contains a sampling of special knots. They are used in numerous tricks throughout the book.

22. Pop-Off Knot

As the audience sees it, the magician ties a knot in the center of a piece of rope. When the ends of the rope are pulled, the knot magically pops off the rope and flies into the air.

Method: Required is a piece of rope about 36" in length and a piece measuring about 6" in length. Arrange them as shown in Figure 134. When presenting the trick, hold the ropes as shown in Figure 135. They will appear to be two separate pieces of rope hanging vertically from the hand.

The left thumb holds the short piece against the long piece. End *D* is gripped between the right thumb and first finger. The right first finger pushes the center of the long piece over the center of

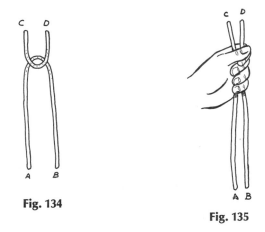

Fig. 134

Fig. 135

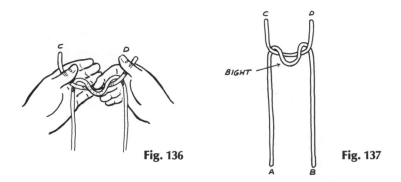

Fig. 136   **Fig. 137**

the short piece as shown in the exposed view of Figure 136. You may find it easier to perform this action with the left first finger. The situation with the hands removed is shown in Figure 137. A bight or loop has been formed in the long piece.

The hands now knot the short piece around the bight. Display the rope as indicated in Figure 138. It appears as if you tied the two ropes together.

Say the magic word, "popcorn," and pull the ends of the rope. The knot will pop off as shown in Figure 139, revealing that two ropes have become one.

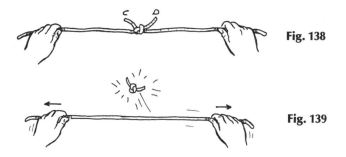

Fig. 138

Fig. 139

23.   The Fake Knot

The magician ties a genuine slip knot in the center of a rope. He then causes the knot to slide off the rope. He bounces the knot off the floor, catches it and drops it in his pocket.

Method: To make the fake knot, tie a knot at the end of a piece of rope as shown in Figure 140. Pull it snug. Cut the knot off. Trim the protruding ends away. The result is the fake knot shown in

Figure 141. To keep the knot from unraveling with use, you can make it more secure by coating it with a clear or white glue. Have one such knot in the right jacket pocket at the start of this trick.

Fig. 140   **Fig. 141**

Display a 36" piece of rope. Openly tie a slip knot in the center of the rope and pull the knot snug. Reach into the right jacket pocket with the right hand for "woofle dust." Sprinkle the invisible dust on the slip knot. Wait a few seconds, then shake the head to indicate it did not work.

Reach into the pocket for more dust. Sprinkle it on the slip knot. Again indicate with a shake of the head it did not work. Reach into the pocket once more. This time bring out the fake knot in the right palm. Do not let the audience see the fake knot.

Sprinkle the woofle dust on the slip knot. Nod the head as if satisfied that the magic has worked. Slide the right hand down the rope, Figure 142, dissolving the slip knot in the process.

When the right hand has slid off the rope, open the hand to display the fake knot. The knot has apparently slid right off the rope. Toss the knot in the air and catch it. If the fake knot is springy enough, you can bounce it off the floor and catch it. Drop it into the pocket and take your bow.

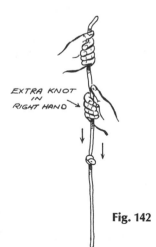

EXTRA KNOT
IN
RIGHT HAND

Fig. 142

24.   Sliding Knot

The magician shows two ropes of equal length. He knots them together. Then he causes the knot to slide down one rope to a point near the bottom. The ropes are untied at that point, showing that one rope is now more than four times longer than the other.

Method: Required are a 36″ length and an 8″ length of rope. Loop the short piece around the center of the long rope as shown in Figure 143.

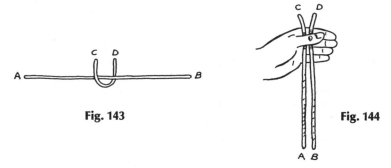

Fig. 143

Fig. 144

To present the routine, hold the ropes as shown in Figure 144. It appears as if you have two ropes of equal length. Knot the short piece around the long piece, Figure 145, and pull the knot snug.

Hold the rope by end A with the left hand. Say, "The ropes are equal. To make them unequal, we move the middle." The right hand then slides the knot down to a point about 4″ from the bottom as shown in Figure 146.

Turn the long rope end for end and hold the knotted portion in the left hand. Untie the knot with the aid of the right hand. Clip

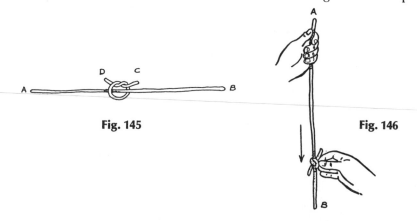

Fig. 145

Fig. 146

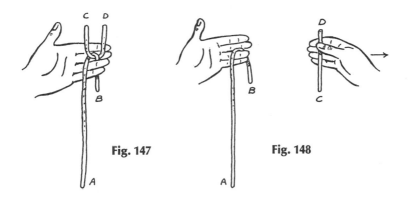

Fig. 147   Fig. 148

end *B* between the left second and third fingers. The position is shown in the exposed view of Figure 147. In practice, the left hand would be closed in a loose fist.

Take end *D* in the right hand. Separate the hands. The result is shown in Figure 148. One rope is now more than four times the length of the other.

25. Here, Spot!

The magician says that he once had a magical dog named Spot. As the magician speaks, he knots a loop in the center of a piece of rope, remarking that the loop was the dog collar and the rope was the leash.

Since Spot knew sleight of hand, he could run off whenever he wanted. The magician tugs on the rope and, as shown in Figure 149, the loop visibly detaches itself from the rope!

Method: This trick uses a fake slip knot. Required is a piece of rope about 36″ long and an extra loop of rope, Figure 150. The extra loop is made by securing the ends of a 6″ piece together with tape or glue to form a loop about 2″ in diameter.

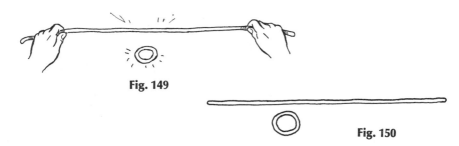

Fig. 149

Fig. 150

The extra loop should be of a size that is easily concealed in the palm, yet large enough to be seen clearly by the audience. The 2" loop is a good size to begin with. If you have trouble concealing it, use a loop of smaller size.

Begin with the extra loop on the center of the rope as shown in Figure 151. Hold the apparatus in the right hand so the extra loop is concealed in the palm. This is the starting position. Note that in Figure 151 the little finger clips the two strands of rope to keep them in place. To present the routine, pull the center of the rope up so it is visible to the audience.

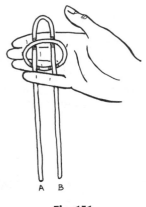

Fig. 151

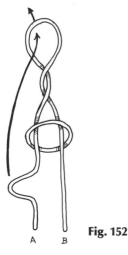

Fig. 152

Give a double twist to the center of the rope. Then pull a strand up through it. This forms the basic slip knot of Figure 152. Tighten the knot by pulling down on end *B*. The situation is shown in Figure 153. The slip knot is visible above the right hand. The extra loop is still concealed in the palm.

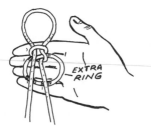

Fig. 153

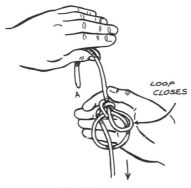

Fig. 154

With the aid of the left hand, fold the genuine slip knot into the right palm. Close the right hand into a fist. Hold end A of the rope in the left hand. Then pull the right hand downward in the direction of the arrow in Figure 154. This has the effect of closing the slip knot. Continue tightening the slip knot until it is snug.

Now display the rope by holding the ends. It looks as if you have a knotted loop in the center of the rope, Figure 155. Explain that sometimes your dog would slip away. As you speak, pull on the ends of the rope. The loop detaches itself and falls free.

Fig. 155

Flourish Knots

Flourishes have eye appeal and offer a change of pace from a steady progression of tricks. The flourishes in this chapter deal with fancy ways to form knots in a piece of rope. The chapter closes with an excellent example of how a double-knot flourish can produce a spectacular effect.

26. Throw Knot

This is a quick flourish. Hold a rope as shown in Figure 156. With a flip of the right hand, throw or toss a loop in the rope as shown in Figure 157. The loop is thrown from right to left.

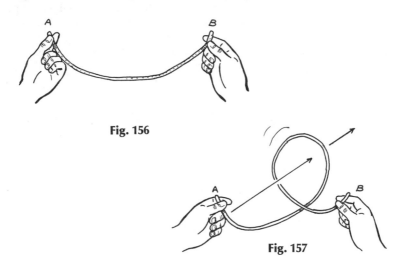

Fig. 156

Fig. 157

While the loop is in the air, slide the left hand through the loop in the direction shown by the arrow in Figure 157. The result is the situation of Figure 158.

Release end *B*. Then grasp end *A* with the right hand and pull the rope off the wrist to show that a genuine knot has formed in the rope.

Patter is to the effect that in cowboy movies they show a cowboy lassoing cattle. Say, "I don't have cattle with me at the moment, but I can illustrate how they do it." Form the knot of Figure 158, then say, "Got him!"

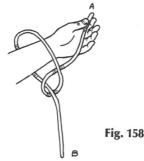

Fig. 158

27.   One-Hand Knot

The magician drapes a piece of rope over his hand. He gives the rope a quick shake and instantly a knot appears in the center of the rope.

The one-hand knot is a classic bit of rope manipulation. The following description, plus the one-hand figure 8 and fake unknot routine, will cover some little-known variations.

Method: The length of rope is not crucial to the handling, but you may want to start with a piece of rope about 40″ long. Drape it over the right hand as shown in Figure 159. One end is clipped between the third and fourth fingers. The other end is draped over the back of the hand. It is important to note that end *B* is closer to the hand than end *A*. The idea is that end *B* must hang so that it can be clipped between the first and second fingers.

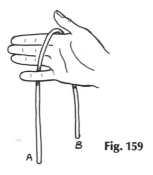

B   **Fig. 159**

Turn the right hand palm down and clip end *B* between the first and second fingers as shown in Figure 160.

Without hesitation, shake or flick the rope off the wrist. The result is that a knot will instantly form in the rope, Figure 161.

When you are familiar with the handling, you will be able to form the knot in a quick, continuous motion. The knot seems to shake itself onto the rope. Learn to tie the one-hand knot with either hand.

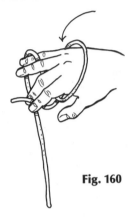

Fig. 160

Fig. 161

28.   Self-Taught Ropes

If you learn to do the one-hand knot with each hand, you can perform an amusing trick. Get two pieces of rope, each measuring about 40″ in length. Have the spectator examine them. Then take a rope in each hand. Step behind the spectator. As soon as the ropes are out of the spectator's sight, tie a one-hand knot in each. Then drape the ropes over his shoulders, Figure 162.

Fig. 162

Ask him to knot the visible ends of the ropes, a knot in each. When he has done this, say, "These are self-taught ropes. They watched the way you tied those knots. Now they can do it themselves."

Have the spectator remove the knotted ropes from his shoulders. He should be surprised to discover that each rope has apparently tied a knot in itself.

29.   One-Hand Figure 8

If you perform the one-hand knot and someone says he knows it, you can switch to a knot that should fool him. The procedure looks almost the same, but you end with a figure 8.

Drape a rope over the right hand as shown in Figure 163. One end of the rope is clipped between the third and fourth fingers. The other end is draped over the back of the hand. This is exactly the starting position for the one-hand knot. The change in handling is as follows.

Remark that you want to adjust the ends. Pull down on end *B* with the left hand, Figure 163, until it hangs lower than end *A*. Note that it crosses end *A* as well.

Turn the right hand palm down and clip end *A* between the first and second fingers as shown in Figure 164.

Fig. 163

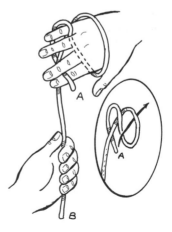

Fig. 164

Shake or flick the rope off the wrist. The result is the figure 8 shown in Figure 165.

Fig. 165

30.   Fake Unknot

After a knot has been tied in the rope by the one-hand method, pull it snug to show it is a genuine knot. Then place it into the right hand as shown in Figure 166. You are going to seem to untie the knot, but in fact the knot will be undisturbed during the untying process.

Method: Having tied the knot, grasp the top of strand *B* between the left thumb and first finger. Tug it upward, Figure 167, as if you were pulling the knot loose. Stop, then tug some more, just as if you were legitimately starting to untie the knot and had to struggle a bit to get it started.

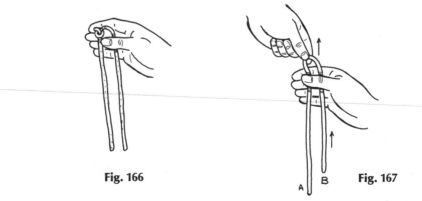

Fig. 166   **Fig. 167**

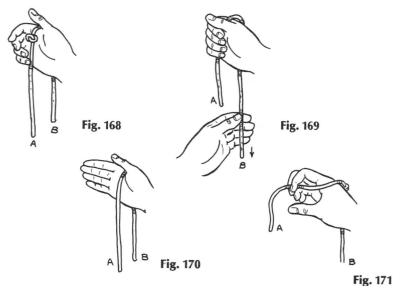

Fig. 168

Fig. 169

Fig. 170

Fig. 171

Continue pulling up a few inches of rope at a time until end *B* is completely free of the right hand. If you have acted the part properly, the audience will be convinced that the knot has been untied. The best way to perform the fake unknot in a natural manner is to study the way you genuinely unknot a rope. You begin in a tentative way, pulling up the loop a bit, then adjusting the grip, then pulling up a bit more. As the knot loosens, your hands move faster, finally causing the knot to dissolve.

As the above method is being enacted, patter that a friend once showed you another method of doing a one-hand knot. Hold the rope in the right hand as shown in Figure 168. The back of the right hand is toward the audience. The fingers are closed. One strand of the rope is between the thumb and first finger and hangs down in back. To the audience, this looks exactly like the starting position for the traditional one-hand knot.

Turn the hand so the fingers are toward the audience. The audience saw you remove a knot from the rope, so they assume the rope has no knots in it at this point. Pull end *B* down, Figure 169, as if to adjust the ends of the rope. Actually, you pull end *B* down just far enough for the knot to slip between the thumb and first finger. At this point, the knot will be at the back of the right hand. Open the right palm, Figure 170. All appears fair. The knot is concealed from audience view because it is behind the right hand.

With the right first and second fingers, grasp end *A* as shown in Figure 171. Snap the rope downward. Instantly, a knot will appear in the center of the rope.

Those who know the traditional method will be fooled by this approach. As a variation, you can use the handling of the one-hand knot to tie a real knot in the rope. The difference is that you will end with two knots.

31. The Double Knot

This clever stunt was invented by D. D. Oeloff. As seen by the audience, the magician makes a quick move and two knots appear in a piece of rope.

Method: Drape the rope over the left hand as shown in Figure 172. Reach through the loop with the right hand. Grasp end *A* and draw it through the loop. Clip it between the left first and second fingers. Then grasp end *B* with the right hand. The situation to this point is shown in Figure 173.

The right thumb and first finger now grasp the loop that is closest to the left thumb, as shown in Figure 174. Lift this loop off the left hand, bringing you to the position shown in Figure 175.

Fig. 172

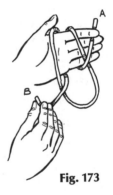

Fig. 173

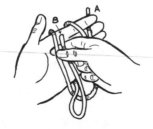

Fig. 174

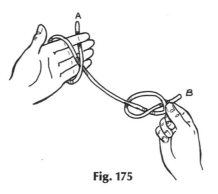

Fig. 175

As soon as the loop clears the left hand, two things are done simultaneously. Flip the loop off the left hand without releasing end *A*. At the same time, release the loop held by the right thumb and first finger without letting go of end *B*. The result will be that two knots form in the rope, Figure 176.

Fig. 176

With practice, you will find it unnecessary to use the right hand to pull the loop off the left hand in Figure 174. When you gain familiarity with the handling, reach the position of Figure 173. Then shake both loops off the left hand with a quick downward motion. Pull the ends apart and the two knots will form as in Figure 176.

32.   Double-Ring Ceremony

In this brilliant routine two borrowed rings are threaded onto a piece of rope. The magician makes a quick move and immediately each ring is tied to the rope with a separate knot.

Although easy to do, this is a spectacular effect that never fails to bring a round of applause.

Method: The trick uses ideas of Zina Bennett, Señor Mardo and Stewart Judah. This handling is based on a description by John Braun.

The rope should be about 40″ long. The method of tying two knots in the rope will be described first.

Hold both ends of the rope in the left hand. The right thumb and first finger are then slipped into the loop at the center of the rope as shown in Figure 177. Raise the right hand to a point at about the center of the two strands and grasp the strands as indicated in Figure 178.

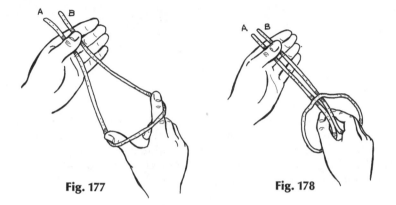

Fig. 177   Fig. 178

Allow the center of the rope to slip off the back of the right hand. Change the right hand's grip so that the right first finger is in front of the strands as shown in Figure 179.

The right thumb and first finger now move up in the direction of the arrow in Figure 179 and grasp end *B*. The position of the right hand at this point is shown in Figure 180.

The left hand retains its grip on end *A*. The right hand holds end *B*. The hands separate. The result is that two knots appear in

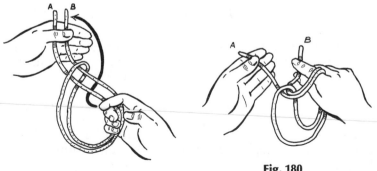

Fig. 179

Fig. 180

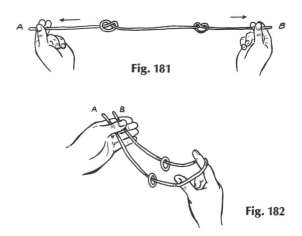

Fig. 181

Fig. 182

the rope as shown in Figure 181. This is a pretty flourish. Practice to get the handling down smoothly. The whole sequence should be done in one continuous motion.

To cause two rings to become knotted on the rope, thread the borrowed rings on. Then grasp the ends with the left hand. The right thumb and first finger enter into the loop at the center of the rope as shown in Figure 182. For the trick to work, there must be a ring on each side of the right hand.

Follow the above handling to form the two knots. When the ends of the rope are pulled apart, each ring will be securely tied with a knot as shown in Figure 183.

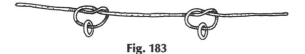

Fig. 183

The trick is much easier to do than it appears to the audience. At times the rings will become tangled in the rope, but that does not take away from the effect. Like the acrobat who fails on the first attempt, the suspense is heightened. Simply start over again. When you reach the situation of Figure 183, the audience will applaud all the louder.

I first saw this routine performed by Don Nielsen. As he did it, the same moves produced no knots, then one knot, then many knots. Don finished with the above trick where two rings became knotted on the rope.

To produce no knots, get the rope to the situation shown in

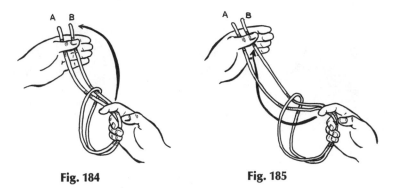

Fig. 184   **Fig. 185**

Figure 179. Then reach *over* the rope in the direction of the arrow shown in Figure 184. Grasp end *B* with the right thumb and first finger. Pull the ends of the rope apart. No knot will form in the rope. Say, "No knot."

Again, get to the position shown in Figure 179. Then reach *through* the center loop in the direction of the arrow shown in Figure 185. Pull the ends apart. As the knot forms, say, "One knot."

Once more get to the configuration shown in Figure 179. This time, reach through the rope in the direction of the arrow shown in Figure 179, but grasp end *A*. Retain the grip on end *B* with the left hand and the grip on end *A* with the right hand. Pull the ends apart. The result will be a tangled knot. Say, "Many knots."

Untangle the rope. Say, "It's easy to produce knots. Kids do it all the time when they tie their shoes. The hard part is to tie a knot at an exact spot in a piece of rope."

Here you borrow two rings, thread them on the rope and proceed with "Double-Ring Ceremony." You end as shown in Figure 183. Not only did you cause two knots to appear in the rope, but they appeared at the exact location of the rings.

Dissolving Knots

In the dissolving knot effect, a seemingly genuine knot, securely tied in the center of a piece of rope, is made to dissolve into nothingness slowly and visibly. In the best such tricks, like the Pretzel Knot described in this chapter (No. 37), the knot can be pulled tighter and tighter; at the last second the knot vanishes.

The closing trick in this chapter is a clever and different routine with dissolving knots.

33.   Not Knot

The magician forms a tangled knot in a piece of rope. When the ends of the rope are pulled, the knot grows tighter. The rope is given another tug and the knot mysteriously dissolves.

Method: This dissolving knot is based on an idea of Tony Lopilato. Hold the ends of a 40″ piece of rope in the left hand. Slip the right hand through the loop at the center of the rope, Figure 186. Grasp both strands of the rope between the right thumb and fingers, Figure 187.

The loop on the right wrist, shown by the arrow in Figure 187, is allowed to slide off the right hand. This is done by pointing the right hand downward. Gravity and a shake of the wrist will cause

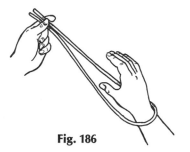

Fig. 186

Fig. 187

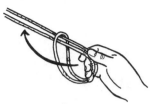

Fig. 188

Fig. 189

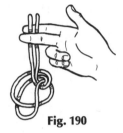

Fig. 190

the loop to slip off the wrist. The position is shown in Figure 188. The left hand still maintains its grip on the ends of the rope.

The right fingers now move in the direction shown by the arrow in Figure 188 and clip the ends of the rope between the right first and second fingers. The result is shown in Figure 189.

The double strand shown by the arrow in Figure 189 is allowed to slide off the right hand. Retain the grip on the ends of the rope. The result is shown in Figure 190.

Take an end of the rope in each hand and gently pull the hands apart. The tangled knot will tighten and then suddenly dissolve.

If the knot dissolves too quickly, when you reach the point of Figure 190 push the knot downward with the left hand. This tightens it up a bit. Then take an end of the rope in each hand and pull the ends apart.

34. Dissolvo

The false knot described in "The Captive Knot" (No. 6) has a number of variations. It can be used in a trick in which you slowly and deliberately tie a genuine knot in a piece of rope, then hypnotize the rope so that, when you tie a knot again, the knot dissolves.

Method: Use a 36″ length of rope. Hold it in the left hand as shown in Figure 191. With the right hand, loop it over the back of the left wrist as shown in Figure 192.

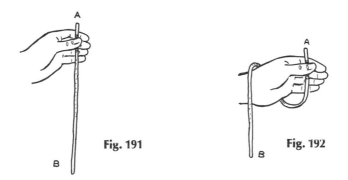

Fig. 191   Fig. 192

The right hand then grasps end *B* and brings it to a position under end *A* as shown in Figure 193. Thread end *A* through the loop in the direction shown by the arrow in Figure 193. This brings you to the position shown in Figure 194.

Without letting go of the ends of the rope, allow the rope to slide off the left wrist. The result is a genuine knot in the center of the rope.

Remark that you will hypnotize the rope so it will not follow commands. Untie the knot. Hold the rope as shown in Figure 191; then get it to the position shown in Figure 192.

Bring end *B* up and over end *A* to the position shown in Figure 195. Thread end *A* through the loop in the direction shown by the arrow in Figure 195. Hold an end of the rope in each hand. The

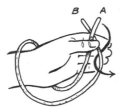

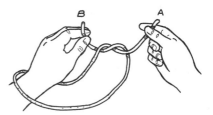

Fig. 193   Fig. 194

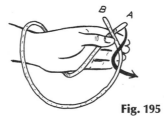

Fig. 195

situation looks almost the same as that shown in Figure 194. Without letting go of the ends of the rope, flip the loop off the left wrist so it falls onto the knot. Then pull the ends of the rope apart. The knot will dissolve.

If you reach the point of Figure 195 and tie the knot indicated by the arrow, you can hand the ends of the rope to the spectator. Although the knot was false when *you* held the ends, the knot becomes genuine when *he* holds the ends. Thus a suspicious spectator can pull the ends of the rope and the knot will not dissolve.

35.   Pull-Away Knot

This is an easy method of tying an apparently real knot that will dissolve when the rope is tightened.

Drape the rope over the hand as shown in Figure 196. The palm of the left hand is toward the audience. Draw both ends through as shown in Figure 197. Place the ends between the left first and second fingers, Figure 198.

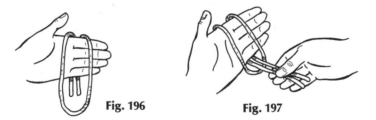

Fig. 196   Fig. 197

Allow the rope to slip off the left hand. Retain the grip on the ends as you do this. The result will be a knot that looks genuine, Figure 199.

Fig. 198

Fig. 199

Take an end of the rope in each hand and slowly draw the ends apart. The knot will tighten and then dissolve.

You can follow this with "The Double Knot" (No. 31). The handling looks the same, but instead of a dissolving knot, you end with two genuine knots in the rope.

36. Posi-Negative Knots

The magician forms a knot in a piece of rope, saying, "This is a positive knot." He forms the knot several times so the audience can see how it is done. Then he forms a positive knot and says, "I'll leave the positive knot in the rope and form a negative knot." He forms the negative knot. When the rope is shaken, positive and negative have canceled one another; now there are no knots in the rope.

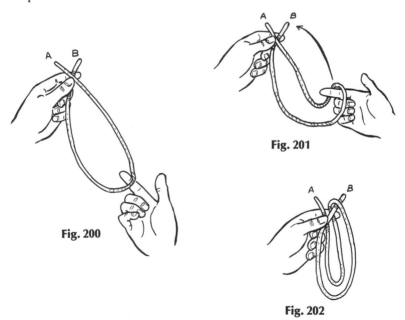

Fig. 200

Fig. 201

Fig. 202

Method: Use a rope about 44″ in length. Cross one end over the other and hold the crossed ends in the left hand as shown in Figure 200. The right first finger catches the center of the rope and brings it upward as shown in the direction of end *B* in Figure 200.

Loop the center of the rope over end *B* as indicated by the arrow in Figure 201. The result is the situation of Figure 202. Take end *B* in the right hand. Hold end *A* in the left hand. Separate the hands and a knot will form in the rope. Magically, the knot seems to drop onto the center of the rope.

Untie the knot. Then repeat the knot two or three times, showing the audience how you tie a positive knot. With all knots untied, form the positive knot one more time. You are at the position of Figure 202. Then transfer the rope to the right hand.

The left first finger grasps the leftmost loop at the bottom and brings it over end *A* by taking it up in the direction of the arrow shown in Figure 203. Remark that this is a negative knot.

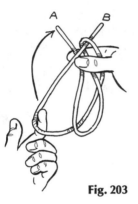

Fig. 203

Take end *A* in the left hand, end *B* in the right hand, and draw the ends apart. The knots cancel one another, leaving you with no knots in the rope.

37. Pretzel Knot

This is one of the most convincing methods for the trick in which a knot formed in the center of a rope seems to fade away as the ends of the rope are pulled. The knot is clearly in view until the last second.

Method: Hold a 40" piece of rope as shown in Figure 204. Bring the right hand behind the left hand, Figure 205. Then bring end *B* into the left palm so it crosses the other strand as shown in Figure 206. End *B* is clipped between the left first and second fingers to hold it in place.

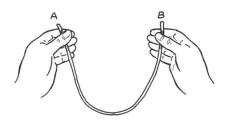

Fig. 204

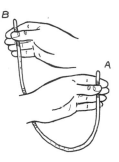

Fig. 205

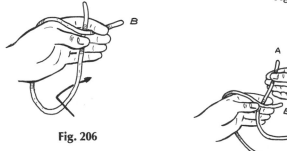

Fig. 206

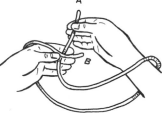

Fig. 207

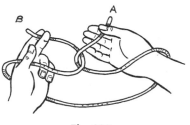

Fig. 208

The right hand is brought through the loop in the direction of the arrow shown in Figure 206. The right hand then grasps end *A* as shown in Figure 207.

The left first and second fingers bring end *B* to the left as shown in Figure 208. Then end *B* is taken between the left thumb and first finger. This is a crucial point in the handling. Note that the rope is still draped over the left hand and right wrist. You are

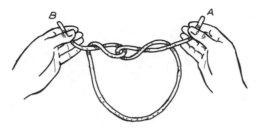

Fig. 209

Fig. 210

going to slide the rope off the hands, but it must be done gently so that the strands fall onto the rope as shown in Figure 209.

Once this has been done, the thumbs twirl the rope in the direction of the arrows shown in Figure 210. The center of the rope will twist back onto itself. As the rope is twirled, pull the ends apart.

The apparent knot in the center will tighten until the last second. Then the knot will magically dissolve.

When going from Figure 208 to Figure 209, if you have trouble keeping the strands in place, twist them in the direction of the arrows shown in Figure 210 just enough to keep them secure. Then slip the strands off the left hand and right wrist. Proceed from here with the handling described above.

38.   Triplicity

A strong opening trick gets the audience's attention. In this routine, the magician holds a piece of rope between his hands. He gives the rope a twist and three knots suddenly appear on the rope.

The magician blows on one knot, causing it to vanish. He unties another knot to show that it is genuine. Then he causes the third knot to slide off the rope.

Method: This trick is based on an original opening routine of Milbourne Christopher's. A simplified version was described in Triple Knots (No. 4). The knot-tying method is one used by Zina Bennett.

To prepare for the routine, use a piece of rope about 40″ long. Take a short piece of rope and tie a snug knot around the long rope about 6″ from one end. Trim the ends of the knot. Then tie a slip knot (see No. 8) about 6″ from the other end of the long rope. The prepared rope is shown in Figure 211. There is a slip knot 6″ from end *A* and a fake knot 6″ from end *B*.

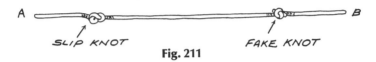

A ——————————————————————— B

SLIP KNOT   FAKE KNOT

Fig. 211

To present the routine, hold the rope as in Figure 212. The backs of the hands are toward the audience. The thumbs conceal the knots.

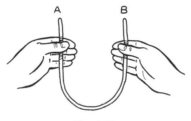

A   B

Fig. 212

Place end *B* into the left hand so it goes under end *A*. This is shown in Figure 213. An exposed view is shown in Figure 214.

B   A

Fig. 213

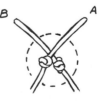

B   A

Fig. 214

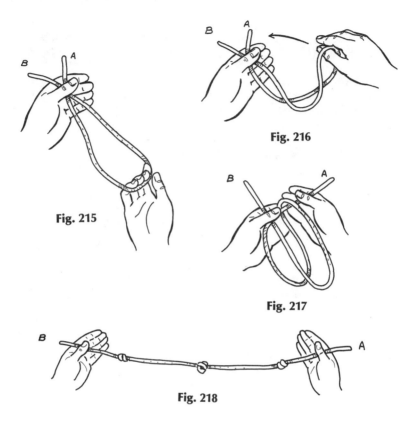

Fig. 216

Fig. 215

Fig. 217

Fig. 218

Turn the right hand palm up. Place it under the center of the rope. The position is indicated in Figure 215. Bring the right hand up to the left hand. As you do, turn the right hand palm down, Figure 216.

Place the loop over end A. Then grasp end A with the right hand as shown in Figure 217. Separate the hands. At the same time make a slight tossing motion as if to toss the center of the rope into the air. The result is shown in Figure 218. It appears as if three knots tied themselves in the rope.

Place the hands on either side of the slip knot. Blow on the knot. At the same time, pull the hands apart, causing the knot to dissolve. Untie the center knot to show that it is genuine. Then blow on the fake knot. Nothing happens. Tug on the rope. Again nothing happens. Finally snap the fingers and slide the knot off the rope.

Toss the knot into the air, catch it and drop it into the pocket. You can now use the rope for further mysteries.

39.   The Penrose Knot

This clever routine was invented by Roger Penrose. The magician ties a series of knots in a rope. Only one of the knots is genuine. The spectator freely chooses one knot, signifying his choice by grasping the knot with thumb and first finger.

The rope is pulled. All of the knots dissolve except the one chosen by the spectator.

Method: Use a 7′ length of rope. You are going to form a chain stitch in the rope. To begin, tie an overhand knot as shown in Figure 219. Then bring end X up to the position shown in Figure 220.

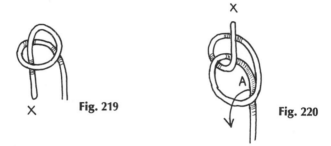

Fig. 219   Fig. 220

Pull the shaded portion A down in the direction shown by the arrow in Figure 220. The rope will now look as shown in Figure 221-A. Bring the shaded portion down in the direction shown by the arrow in Figure 221-A. The rope will then look as shown in Figure 221-B. Now bring the shaded portion down in the direc-

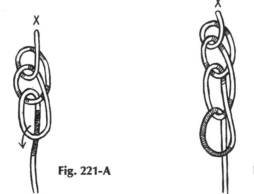

Fig. 221-A   Fig. 221-B

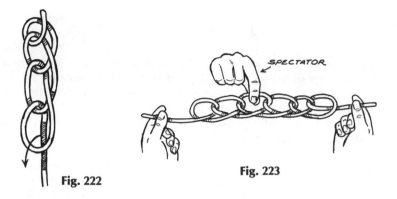

Fig. 222

Fig. 223

tion of the arrow shown in Figure 222. Continue doing this until you reach a point near the bottom of the rope.

The above preparation can be done beforehand. The prepared rope can be placed on the table. When you are ready to perform the trick, take the rope from the table, holding it at the ends. Explain that there are a series of slip knots on the rope, but that one knot is genuine.

Have the spectator choose a loop by grasping it between thumb and first finger, Figure 223. Then pull the ends of the rope in opposite directions as shown by the arrows in Figure 224.

The result is that the chain will dissolve, leaving a genuine overhand knot in the rope at exactly the point chosen by the spectator, Figure 224.

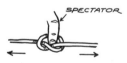

Fig. 224

Cut-and-Restored Rope

In *The Discoverie of Witchcraft* Reginald Scot explained for the first time the secret of how "To cut a lace asunder in the middest, and to make it whole againe." After explaining the method, he concludes, "This, if it be well handled, will seeme miraculous."

In the centuries since, hundreds of cut-and-restored-rope tricks have appeared in print. Dariel Fitzkee provided a succinct analysis of the basic principles in *The Only Six Ways to Restore a Rope* (1944):

> So here we have the cut and restored rope trick dissected into its components. We find the some hundred odd rope restorations resolving to three elements. Strangely these three integrants are almost synonymous with the constituents of all forms of low cunning. Disguise. Pretense. Substitution.

This chapter contains examples of some of the basic principles used to perform the trick where a rope is visibly cut into pieces and then restored. Most of the methods are impromptu and can be performed either close up or from the stage.

40. Vishnu Rope Mystery

In this fine trick, based on a routine invented by Bob Ellis, a rope is openly cut into three pieces. The pieces are knotted together. On command, the three pieces join to become a solid rope.

There are no gimmicks. The rope may be examined before and after the trick is performed.

Method: The rope should be about 6' long. Hold one end clipped between the left first and second fingers. The right hand holds a pair of scissors. Open the scissor blades and engage the rope near the left hand at the point marked *C* in Figure 225.

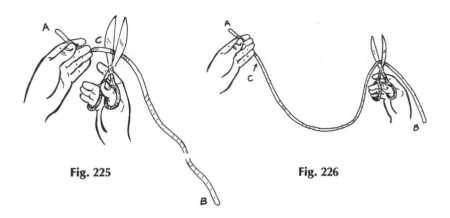

Fig. 225   **Fig. 226**

Slide the scissors out to a position about a third of the way from the opposite end of the rope as shown in Figure 226. Bring this portion up over the left palm, then drape it over the left second, third and fourth fingers, Figure 227. Slide the scissors down and off the rope. With a continuing motion, pick up the rope at the point marked *C* in Figure 228. This is the same point *C* shown in Figure 225.

Lift this portion up to the position shown in Figure 229. Hold it in place with the left thumb. Cut the rope at *C*, allowing the long end to fall. The result is the situation shown in Figure 230. It appears as if the rope was fairly cut a third of the way from end *B*

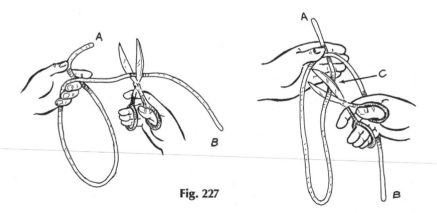

Fig. 227

Fig. 228

but the point marked *C* in Figure 229 is the same as the point marked *C* in Figure 226, so the rope was actually cut near end *A*.

Tie *A–C* into a knot around the rope as indicated in Figure 231. If you make the motion of sliding the scissors along the rope and then picking up the rope at *C* smoothly, the audience will be convinced that the rope has been fairly cut. Additional cover for the deception can be obtained if you make sure the back of the left hand is toward the audience when you pick up the rope at *C* in Figure 228.

Grasp the rope at end *D* with the left hand. Then slide the scissors down until they are about a third of the way from the opposite end, Figure 232. Lift this portion of the rope and bring it

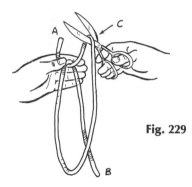

Fig. 229

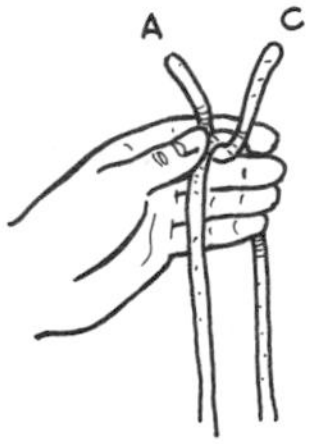

Fig. 230

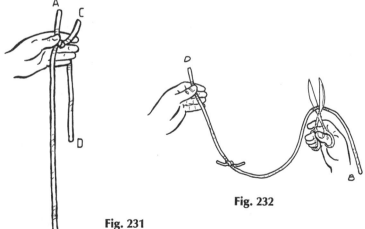

Fig. 231

Fig. 232

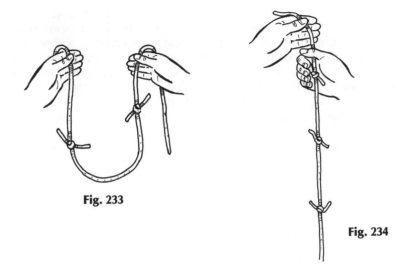

Fig. 233

Fig. 234

over to the left palm. Then repeat all of the action depicted in Figures 227–231 to cut the rope and tie the ends. Put the scissors in the pocket. The result is that you apparently hold three pieces of rope knotted together as shown in Figure 233.

Grasp the rope with the right hand at a point just below the left hand, Figure 234. Loop the rope over the left fingers in the direction shown by the arrows in Figure 235. Continue looping the rope over the left hand. As you do, the knots will slide down the rope. At the finish, when all of the rope has been wound around the left fingers, the knots will slide off the rope and will be concealed in the right hand as shown in Figure 236.

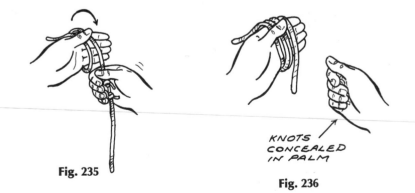

KNOTS
CONCEALED
IN PALM

Fig. 235

Fig. 236

Place the right hand in the pocket. Leave the knots behind. Take out the scissors and wave them over the rope. Then catch one end of the rope between the scissor blades and separate the hands, Figure 237, to show the rope restored.

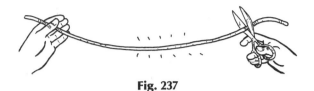

Fig. 237

41. Impey's Impromptu

Eric Impey devised an ingenious method for the cut-and-restored rope trick. The following routine is based on his handling.

Method: The rope is about 50″ in length. Make a pencil dot at the center of the rope so it can be spotted as an easy reference point later on. Hold the rope in the right hand near one end as shown in Figure 238.

Grasp the rope a few inches below the center with the left thumb and first finger. Drape this portion of the rope over the right second, third and fourth fingers as shown in Figure 239. Curl these fingers around the rope.

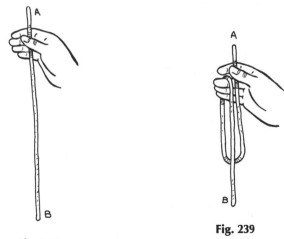

Fig. 239

Fig. 238

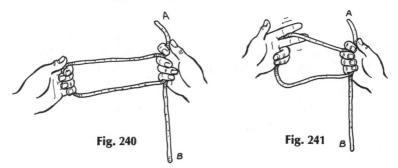

Fig. 240   Fig. 241

The left fingers then pull the center loop taut, as shown in Figure 240. As this is done, turn so the backs of the hands are toward the audience.

Say, "If I cut the rope here——." At this point release the left hand's grip and immediately clip the rope at the center between the left first and second fingers, Figure 241, as if these fingers were a pair of scissors.

Release the right hand's grip on the rope. Say, "The rope would be cut in two equal pieces." The audience can see that the rope is clipped between the left first and second fingers at the center.

Act satisfied that you were able to estimate the center of the rope accurately. Invite a spectator up to cut the rope. You now apparently go back to the beginning but there is a subtle difference in the handling.

Hold the rope between the right thumb and first finger but with the rope going behind the right second, third and fourth fingers as shown in Figure 242. Keep the palm of the right hand toward the audience.

Grasp the rope a few inches below center between the left thumb and first finger. Drape this portion of the rope over the right second, third and fourth fingers exactly as shown in Figure 243. Note that this is opposite to the way it was done in Figure 239.

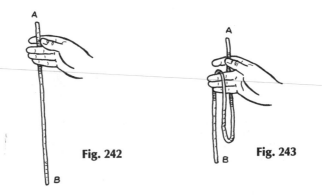

Fig. 242   Fig. 243

Curl the right second, third and fourth fingers inward around the rope. The left hand then pulls the center loop taut, as shown in Figure 244. At the same time extend the backs of the hands to the audience. This looks like the situation shown in Figure 240, but is different. If the spectator cuts the rope at the point indicated in Figure 244, he will not be cutting the center of the rope. Rather, he will be cutting the rope at a point near end *A*.

After the rope has been cut, release the left hand's grip. The rope will appear as in Figure 245. Take the scissors from the spectator. Trim away all of the segment *A–C* by snipping small portions and letting them fall to the floor.

Stretch the rope between the hands to show that it is fully restored.

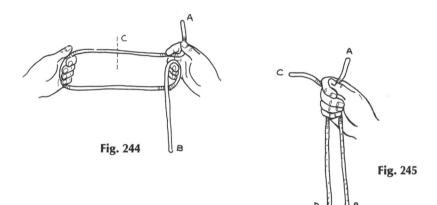

Fig. 244

Fig. 245

42. Karl Germaine's Method

Early in this century Karl Germaine devised a method for cutting and restoring a rope that depended on the idea of disguising the rope so that the ends appeared to be the center. Thus, while apparently cutting through the center of the rope, the magician was really cutting through the ends. The rope could then be shown to have apparently restored itself.

Method: The trick requires a prepared rope. Take a piece of white rope about 40″ in length. Tape the ends together by placing the ends against one another and winding adhesive tape around them.

Fig. 246

Fig. 247

Fig. 248

Then place a 6″ piece of rope around the center of the loop. The result is shown in Figure 246.

If the rope is held as shown in Figure 247, it appears as if the left hand holds the ends. At a distance of six feet the tape cannot be spotted. The result is that the rope seems unprepared.

Cut the rope at the apparent center, as shown in Figure 247. Then trim the cut ends until all of the tape has been trimmed away. Tie the upper ends of the rope together. Then tie the lower ends of the rope together. Display the rope as shown in Figure 248.

Run the rope through the hands so that the audience does not have a clear idea which ends are which. Then pick up the scissors and trim away the 6″ piece of rope. Finish by untying the other ends and showing the rope completely restored. Toss the rope to the audience for examination.

As an alternative approach, you can tie the 6″ piece to the long rope by means of a pop-off knot (No. 22). Display the rope as shown in Figure 248. Run the rope through the hands so the audience loses track of which part of the rope you have cut. Then hold the rope as shown in Figure 248 again, with the pop-off knot uppermost. Pull the hands apart sharply and the upper knot flies off. Untie the rope and toss it to the audience for examination.

43.   Hindu Turban Mystery

In this spectacular mystery, a long piece of rope is stretched out to its full length and is held in place by two spectators. The magician cuts the rope into two equal pieces, then instantly restores the rope.

In part the mystery gains strength from the fact that the rope is so long it seemingly cannot be manipulated by the magician. The entire length of rope is always in view, there are no gimmicks and a spectator genuinely cuts the rope.

Method: This handling is derived from the routine used by J. W. Sarles. The rope can be 8′ or longer. In the following illustrations, the magician's hands are those protruding from jacket sleeves. The other hands are those of volunteer spectators.

Ask two spectators to participate. Each takes an end of the rope. Have the spectators back away from one another so the rope is stretched out to its full length. Stand so the rope is between you and the audience.

Slide the palm-up left hand along the rope. Say, "In some Eastern cultures, there is the belief that life stretches out along a straight path like this rope."

Stop when you reach the center of the rope, Figure 249. Have the spectator on your right give you his end of the rope. This is end *B* shown in Figure 249. Take end *B* and place it in the left hand so it marks the center of the rope. With the right hand, hold up a strand so that a loop is displayed, Figure 250. Call attention to the loop as you say, "The spirit is seen as a circle."

Note that in Figure 250 the rope is held between the left second and third fingers. This is important to the handling. The left hand is shown open in Figure 250 only to expose the left hand's grip. In practice, the hand would be closed in a loose fist.

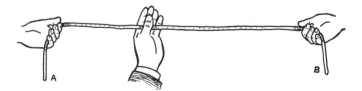

Fig. 249

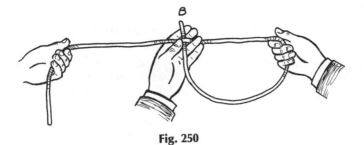

Fig. 250

Release the right hand's grip, allowing the rope to fall to the position shown in Figure 251. Say, "The center of the rope represents the center of existence, where the physical and the mental achieve balance." Point to the center of the rope with the right first finger. You seem to have released the right hand's grip on the loop shown in Figure 250 because you wanted to point to the center of the rope.

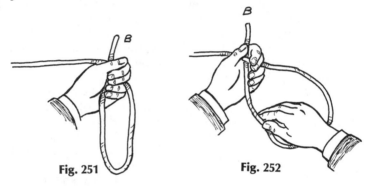

Fig. 251   **Fig. 252**

Regrip the rope at the point shown in Figure 252, that is, at a point just below the left hand. Bring the rope up to the right to form a loop again. To the audience this appears to be the same situation shown in Figure 250, but the true situation is indicated in Figure 253. You have switched the center of the rope for the end.

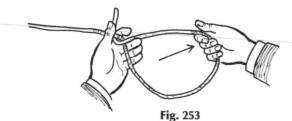

Fig. 253

Say, "Sometimes the smooth journey through life is interrupted. The circle is broken." Have the spectator on your right cut the rope at the point indicated in Figure 254. He thinks he is cutting the center, but he is really cutting a point near end *B*.

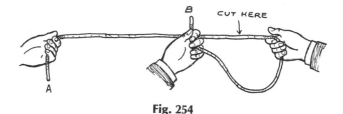

Fig. 254

After the spectator cuts the rope, release the right hand's grip. The rope falls to the position shown in Figure 255. Hand end *D* to the spectator on your right and have him step back to his original position so the rope is taut again. Do not release the left hand's grip on the rope.

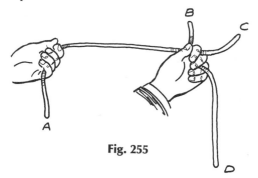

Fig. 255

Tie ends *B* and *C* together. This produces the knotted rope shown in Figure 256. Say, "Life becomes tangled in knots. We lose our way."

Take the scissors with the right hand. Hold the knot with the left hand. Begin trimming the knot as you say, "In these situations, the thing to do is to simplify. Trim away the excess and only the essence remains."

Fig. 256

By this time, you have trimmed away all of the knot. Release the left hand from the rope and step back. The rope is now entirely restored.

The trick gets its name from the fact that it is sometimes performed with a wide cloth which the magician says is used to make a turban. The turban is unwound and stretched out across the stage. The trick then commences as described above.

44.   Scissorcut

This amusing trick was devised by Martin Gardner. A pair of scissors is threaded onto a piece of rope. The spectator holds the ends of the rope. The scissors are covered with a handkerchief. Reaching under the handkerchief, the magician releases the scissors in the most obvious way, by cutting the rope with the scissors, removing the scissors, then tying the ends of the rope.

When the spectator objects that this is not much of a trick, the magician slides the knot off the rope, thus magically restoring the rope.

Method: Thread the end of a 40″ piece of rope through the left handle of a pair of scissors, then around the blades and back through the same handle as shown in Figure 257. Continue by threading the end of the rope through the right handle, Figure 258, then around the blades and back through the right handle, Figure 259. The scissors appear to be genuinely threaded onto the rope at this point. The spectator takes one end of the rope in each hand.

In the pocket is a handkerchief and a rope segment measuring

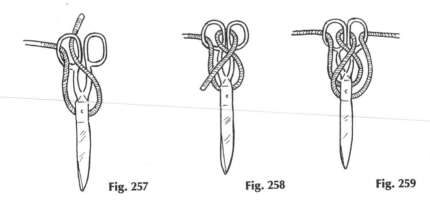

Fig. 257   Fig. 258   Fig. 259

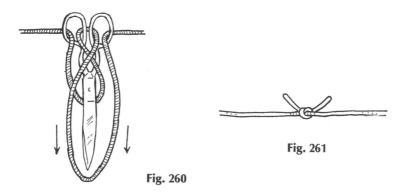

Fig. 261

Fig. 260

about 3″ in length. Grasp the rope segment in the hand, then take the handkerchief on top of it so the rope segment is hidden.

Drape the handkerchief over the rope so the scissors are hidden from view. There are two loops around the blades of the scissors. Draw one down in the direction of the arrow shown in Figure 260 until it is off the blades. Then draw the other loop down and off the blades. The scissors are now free of the rope.

Hold the scissors in place with the left little finger. Then tie the short segment of rope around the center of the rope held by the spectator. Remove the scissors and display them.

With a flourish remove the handkerchief from the rope. The audience is greeted with the sight of a rope that has apparently been cut in two and then knotted, Figure 261. When the spectator remarks that the stunt is not magical, pretend to notice the knot for the first time. Wave the scissors over the knot, then slide the knot off the rope. The rope has been magically restored.

45. Knot at All

The magician openly ties a knot in the center of a piece of rope. The spectator cuts the knot off the rope, thus severing the rope into two equal parts.

The rope is magically restored. For a novel finish, the knot mysteriously appears back on the center of the rope.

Method: This routine is based on an idea of Dr. Weiner. The only requirement is a 42″ piece of rope, a pair of scissors and a paper bag.

Beforehand, tie a knot about 6″ from one end of the rope. With a pen or pencil place a dot about 18″ from the knot. The pencil dot

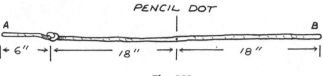

Fig. 262

will aid in positioning another knot in the rope later on. The prepared rope is shown in Figure 262. The rope and scissors are placed in the paper bag.

To present the trick, open the bag and place it upright on the table. Remove the scissors and place them on the table. Grasp the rope. Hold it between the hands as shown in Figure 263. The knot is concealed in the left palm, near the fingers. The end of the rope is held firmly in place with the left thumb. The rope extends out from between the first and second fingers.

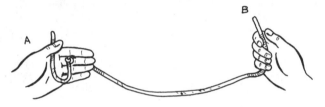

Fig. 263

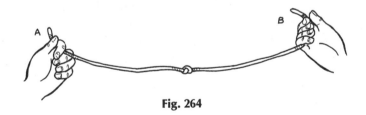

Fig. 264

Hand a pen to the spectator. Ask him to put his initials or some identifying mark near end *B* of the rope. Then take back end *B* and once again hold the rope as shown in Figure 263.

Tie a loose knot in the right end of the rope. After the knot is made, position it where the pencil dot is. The rope now looks as shown in Figure 264. Remark that the knot marks the approximate center of the rope.

The right hand swings the center of the rope to the left, where it is caught between the left third and fourth fingers, Figure 265. Pull the rope to the right until the knot is snug against the left third and fourth fingers, Figure 266.

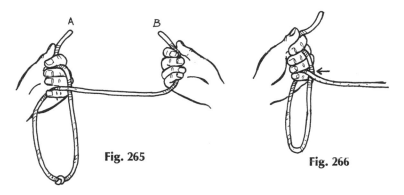

Fig. 265

Fig. 266

The right hand maintains its grip on end B for this next move. The right second and third fingers will now grasp the strand shown by the arrow in Figure 266. The right fingers pull to the right. This is shown in Figure 267. The appearance you want to give is that you will draw the knot out into view.

At the same time, turn to the left to pick up a pair of scissors from the table. This slight turning helps cover the next move. The right fingers continue pulling to the right. In the process they pull the top strand of rope so that the prepared knot comes into view, Figure 268.

Recall that there were a few inches of slack in the rope held by the left hand as shown in Figure 263. The right hand pulls to the right until all of the slack has been taken from the left hand. End A of the rope is still firmly held in place by the left thumb. This end does not move. All the audience sees is that you have pulled the knot into view. It does not realize that this is a different knot from the one it saw in Figure 264.

Fig. 267

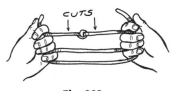

Fig. 268

Hand the scissors to the spectator. Have him cut the rope on each side of the knot, as shown by the arrows in Figure 268. This cuts the knot completely away from the rope.

Release the right hand's grip on the rope.

Take the knot from him and place it into the left palm. Then hand him end *B* of the rope. Ask him to verify his initials. While he holds end *B* firmly, drop the rope into the paper bag. This means that the rope, the knot and a small segment that was once end *A* are dropped into the bag. Shake the bag. Slowly withdraw the rope. Not only has the rope restored itself, the knot is back in place!

46.   Victor Rope Trick

In this contemporary classic a rope is cut into two pieces and restored. At once, the rope is again cut in two pieces and is immediately restored. The ingenious handling allows you to perform this excellent mystery without gimmicks or preparation.

Method: Invented by the British magician Edward Victor and published in 1937, this rope trick contains many features used today. Required is a 48″ length of rope and a pair of scissors. At the start the scissors are in the right jacket pocket.

Stand with the left side to the audience. Grip one end of the rope between the left thumb and first finger. The right hand turns palm up and contacts the rope at a point just above the center. The starting position is shown in Figure 269.

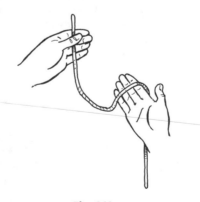

Fig. 269

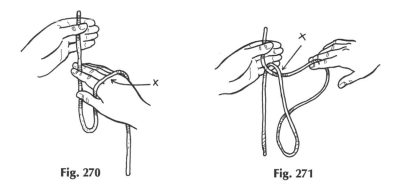

Fig. 270   Fig. 271

Turn the right hand palm down and lift it toward the left hand. The right first and second fingers clip the rope at a point about an inch below the left hand, Figure 270.

Point the right fingers toward the floor and raise the back of the right hand. This allows the rope to slide off the back of the hand. The strand on the back of the right hand, labeled X in Figure 270, falls to the position shown in Figure 271.

The loop clipped between the right first and second fingers is placed against the left fingers. It is held in place with the left thumb, Figure 272.

The right hand now takes the scissors from the pocket and cuts the loop at the point shown in Figure 272. To the audience it appears as if you are cutting the center of the rope, but, as shown in the exposed view of Figure 273, you are really cutting the rope at a position near the upper end.

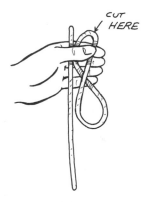

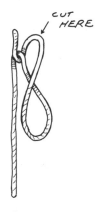

Fig. 272   Fig. 273

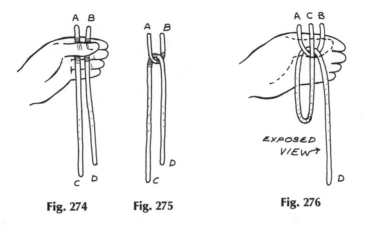

Fig. 274   Fig. 275   Fig. 276

As soon as the rope is cut, allow the outer strand to fall free of the left thumb. This produces the situation shown in Figure 274. It appears as if the rope has been cut into two strands. The true situation is shown in an exposed view, Figure 275. The back of the left hand is toward the audience and acts to screen the true situation from audience view.

Remark that the two pieces are not of equal length so you will have to start over. The right hand brings end C up to a point between A and B, Figure 276.

Then the right hand brings end D to the right of end B. The four ends are held in place with the left thumb, Figure 277. The right hand then grasps end D between the thumb and first finger, Figure 278. The right hand turns palm down and grasps end B between the thumb and first finger, Figure 279.

The right hand moves to the right. The left hand releases end A, but it maintains contact on end C. The hands stretch apart, revealing that the rope has restored itself, Figure 280. This is a strong and surprising effect.

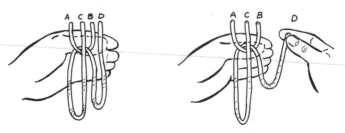

Fig. 277   Fig. 278

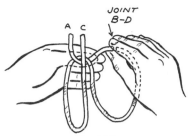

Fig. 279

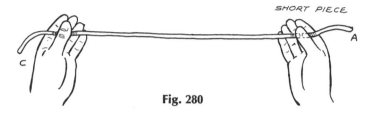

Fig. 280

Say, "Let's start again." The right hand brings end *A* to the left and places it on top of the strand held by the left hand. End *A* is held in place by the left thumb, Figure 281. Unknown to the audience, the right hand does not hold a single solid strand of rope. Rather, it holds the bottom of the short piece (end *B*) and the top of the long piece (end *D*) as shown in the exposed view of Figure 282.

To the audience, it looks as if you are going to loop end *C* around the strand in the right hand and then tie a knot. In fact, because of clever handling, end *C* will be switched for end *B*. Begin by grasping end *C* with the left thumb and second finger.

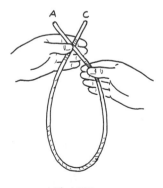

Fig. 281

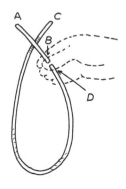

Fig. 282

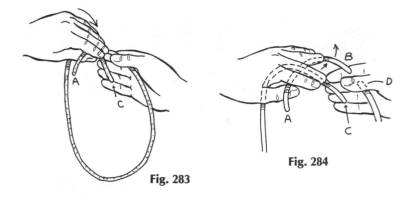

Fig. 284

Fig. 283

Pivot end *C* around and into the right palm, Figure 283. Make sure you place end *C* directly onto the right third and fourth fingers as shown in Figure 283.

The left second and third fingers now clip end *B*. The start of this action is shown in the exposed view of Figure 284. The arrows indicate the direction taken by the left second finger. The right thumb releases pressure on end *B* to allow it to pivot upward. This end is then gripped between the left second and third fingers.

The situation is now shown in the exposed view of Figure 285. In actual performance, the right hand would conceal the true situation from audience view. All it sees is the view shown in Figure 286.

The left hand knots *A* and *B* together and pulls the knot snug but not too tight. The rope is then displayed as shown in Figure 287.

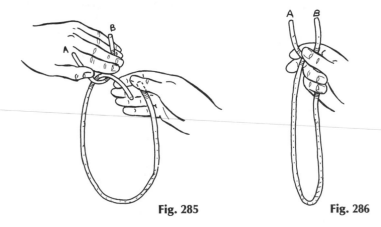

Fig. 285   Fig. 286

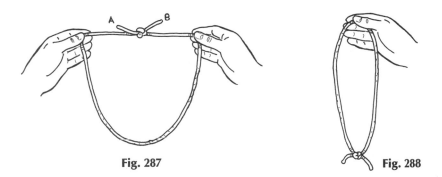

Fig. 287   Fig. 288

Say, "If we bring the ends to the bottom, we'll get the middle on top." Release the left hand's grip on the rope. Then grasp the knot between the left thumb and first finger. Slide it down to the bottom of the rope. It appears as if you are running or sliding the rope through the right hand as you pull the knotted ends downward. The end result is shown in Figure 288. An exposed view is given in Figure 289.

Transfer the rope to the left hand, taking care to keep ends C and D from showing. Then reach into the right jacket pocket and remove the scissors.

Pretend to cut the middle of the rope at the center. As you do, simply release end D, allowing it to fall. This produces the illusion that the rope was cut at the center. The result is shown in Figure 290.

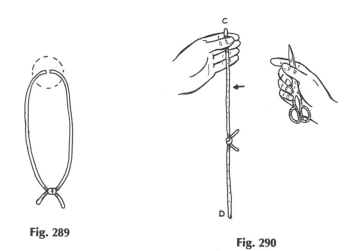

Fig. 289

Fig. 290

Fig. 291   Fig. 292

Say, "The ends still aren't even." Grasp the rope with the right hand at the point shown by the arrow in Figure 290. Place this into the left hand, Figure 291. Do not release the right hand's grip on the rope. Simply slide the right hand down to the knot, Figure 291, and apparently place the knot into the left fist.

Do not release the right hand's grip on the knot. Slide the right hand downward, pulling the knot completely off the rope. The position now is shown in Figure 292. The knot is concealed in the right hand.

Place the scissors and the knot into the right jacket pocket. Say, "Now the rope is restored." Release the rope, holding just end C in the left hand. The rope has restored itself once again. Stretch the rope between the hands, tug on it, then toss it out for examination.

The Hunter Knot

Hold one end of a rope in each hand and do not let go of the ends; it is impossible to tie an overhand knot in the rope. Magicians have devoted much time and study to making the impossible possible, that is, to devise a trick where you seemingly are able to tie an overhand knot without letting go of the ends of the rope.

The British magician G. W. Hunter invented one of the best methods for solving the problem. This chapter describes some of the variations that have been developed since the Hunter knot first appeared. It includes a method in which a genuine knot does in fact appear in the rope without the ends being released.

47. A Possible Impossibility

As seen by the audience, the magician ties a knot in a piece of rope without letting go of the ends of the rope. The trick is repeated several times. Spectators who think they can duplicate the method find that, although they follow the moves exactly, they cannot tie a knot in the rope.

Method: Use a piece of rope about 36″ in length. Hold the rope as shown in Figure 293. Note that each end is held between thumb and first finger. The other fingers are curled in. The right hand holds end *B* of the rope as close to the end as possible.

To form the Hunter knot, bring the right hand to the left and over the left hand, Figure 294. Then bring the right hand

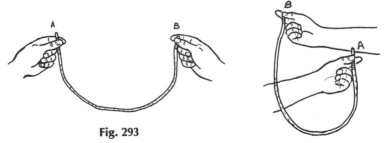

Fig. 293

Fig. 294

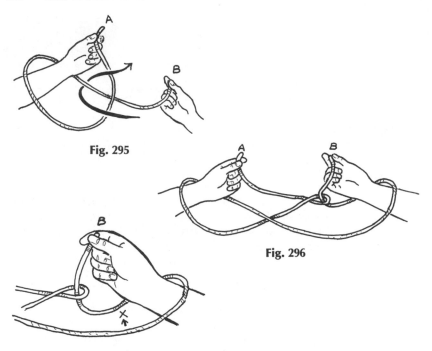

Fig. 295

Fig. 296

Fig. 297

down to the position shown in Figure 295. The right hand then threads through the rope in the direction shown by the arrow in Figure 295.

The situation thus far is shown in Figure 296. To form a genuine knot in the rope, it is necessary to transfer the right hand's grip secretly from end B to point X indicated by the arrow in Figure 297. Simply let go of end B and grasp the rope at the point marked X. Lower the hands to allow the rope to slip off the wrists. You will find that a genuine knot has appeared in the rope.

This is the basic method of forming the Hunter knot. The trick is too obvious if done as described above. For the trick to be deceptive, the transfer of the right hand's grip from B to X must be undetectable. A better handling is as follows.

Note that, to the point indicated in Figure 296, the left hand has remained stationary. When you reach the situation indicated in Figure 296, bring the left hand forward as shown by the arrow in Figure 298. You are going to throw the rope off the left wrist, so it is natural for the left hand to move forward. As the left hand moves, make sure you maintain tension on the rope.

You will find that the point marked X automatically moves to a

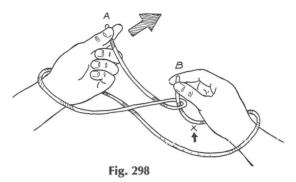

Fig. 298

position close to the right thumb and first finger as the left hand moves forward, Figure 299. When the point marked X contacts the right thumb, it is an easy matter to transfer the right hand's grip from end B to point X.

Once this has been done, the left hand continues its forward motion, eventually throwing the rope off the left wrist. The result is shown in Figure 300; a knot will have formed in the rope.

Practice the above handling so you can do it as a smooth, continuous sequence.

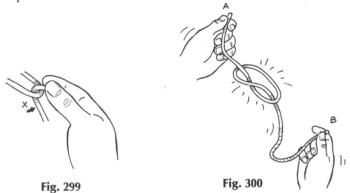

Fig. 299   **Fig. 300**

48.   Fooling the Expert

If you do the Hunter knot several times for the same spectator, he may not see exactly what you do, but he may suspect that you are doing more than you claim. When this happens you can spring the following maneuver on him.

Slowly and deliberately go through the moves that lead you to Figure 296. Ask the spectator if all is fair and aboveboard to this point. He must agree. Say to him, "The knot has already formed in the rope. You can see it for yourself."

Still holding the rope as in Figure 296, say, "At this point I just slip the rope off my wrists. I'll tell you what. This time, you hold the ends of the rope while I slide my hands free. This way I can't do any sleight of hand."

Let the spectator take an end of the rope in each hand. When he has done so, release your grip and slowly slide your hands out of the rope. The spectator pulls the ends of the rope. He will be surprised to see a genuine knot form in the center of the rope.

49.   Neale's Knot

Robert E. Neale devised a subtle variation of the Hunter knot. Hold the rope as shown in Figure 301. Now bring the right hand around behind the left hand as shown in Figure 302. This looks similar to the start of the Hunter knot but it is exactly opposite. Bring the right hand down to its original position. The situation now is as shown in Figure 303.

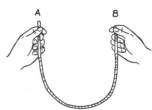

Fig. 301

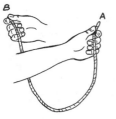

Fig. 302

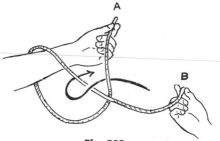

Fig. 303

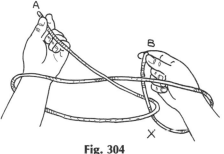

Fig. 304

Thread the right hand through the rope as indicated by the arrow in Figure 303. This brings you to Figure 304. The result will be a situation similar to, but not identical with, Figure 296 of the Hunter knot. Switch end *B* for *X* as described in the Hunter knot. When you shake the rope off the wrists, an overhand knot will form in the rope.

The difference shows up when you give the ends of the rope to the spectator. Go through the sequence of Figures 301–303, then thread the right-hand end through the rope as indicated by the arrow in Figure 303. The result is as indicated in Figure 304.

Hand the ends of the rope to a spectator and slip your hands free. When the spectator pulls the ends of the rope an overhand knot does not form. Instead, a figure-8 knot forms in the rope.

This suggests numerous possibilities. For example, go through the handling of the Hunter knot up to the point shown in Figure 296. Hand the ends of the rope to a man. He takes the rope, pulls the ends apart and an overhand knot forms in the rope.

Go through what seem to be the same motions, but really form the Neale knot up to the point shown in Figure 304. Hand the ends of the rope to a woman. She takes the rope, pulls on the ends and finds that instead of an overhand knot, a figure 8 has appeared in the rope. Remark that men and women have different effects on a piece of rope: With men the rope forms an overhand knot, with women a figure 8.

50.   Double Cross

When many people try to form a genuine knot by following the move of the Hunter knot, they assume that at some point the ends must be switched in order for a knot to form. When they see you perform the Hunter knot several times, they will realize that the ends are not switched. As soon as you see their attention stray from the ends of the rope, you can perform this underhanded variation.

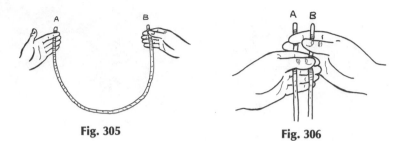

Fig. 305   Fig. 306

Hold the rope as shown in Figure 305. This position is almost the same as that shown in Figure 293, but the left hand grips the rope between the first and second fingers. Note that the ends protrude above the hands.

Follow the steps shown in Figures 293–296. Wiggle the right fourth finger in the direction of the twisted loops near point X in Figure 297, saying, "This is where the knot forms."

Bring the hands together as shown in Figure 306. The back of the left hand touches the right palm. Say to the spectator, "Maybe you can see the knot better from this angle."

Turn the hands palm down, Figure 307. As the hands turn palm down, grip end B with the left thumb and first finger. Simultaneously, grip end A with the right first and second fingers. This exchange of ends must be done while the hands turn to the position shown in Figure 307. When the hands reach that position, the exchange has to be completed.

After giving the spectators a chance to examine the rope in this position, bring the hands to the situation shown in Figure 308. As the hands turn to this position, separate the hands. The ends have been secretly exchanged.

Slowly shake the rope off the wrists. Pull the ends of the rope to show that a tangled but genuine knot has formed in the rope.

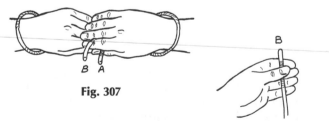

B A

Fig. 307

Fig. 308

51. Hunter Killer

Reserve this method for the occasion when you want to fool a fellow magician who knows how to perform the Hunter knot. It is a version in which a genuine knot appears in the rope, although you do not let go of the ends. The secret lies in the fact that the knot is formed before the trick begins, but the handling is such that the secret knot is never suspected.

Method: Tie a convertible knot (No. 12) about 4″ from the end of a 36″ length of rope. This is the only preparation. The knot should look as shown in Figure 68.

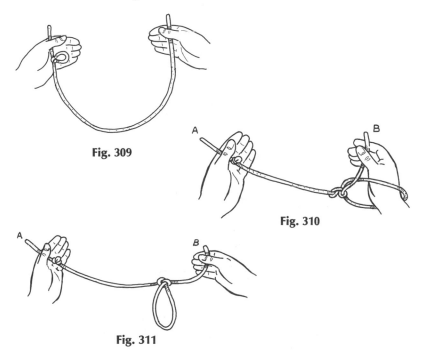

Fig. 309

Fig. 310

Fig. 311

To perform the trick, hold the rope as shown in Figure 309. The knot is concealed in the left palm. Perform all of the moves of the Hunter knot up to the point indicated in Figure 296. Do the moves slowly and deliberately. Then allow the rope to slide off the left wrist. Pull the knot snug as shown in Figure 310. Slowly allow the rope to fall off the right wrist without letting go of end *B*. The situation now is as shown in Figure 311. Pull the ends of the rope so the knot tightens. Make sure you do not pull too hard. You do not want the knot to dissolve. The loop should be the same size as the loop of the knot concealed in the left hand.

Say, "That's it, a genuine knot." As you say this, flip the slip knot into the left fist, Figure 312. Then pull end *B* to the right.

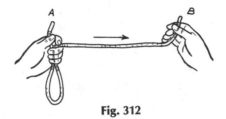

Fig. 312

The slip knot will dissolve in the left fist. Keep pulling the rope to the right, allowing it to slide from the left fingers until the convertible knot is about to be pulled into view. It appears as if the knot is being drawn along the rope toward end *A*.

The spectator will object that you tied only a slip knot. Say, "No, it may look like a slip knot, but it's genuine."

Release end *B*. Then take end *A* with the right hand. Do not open the left fist yet. Pull end *A* up so the knot comes into view. Hand the rope to the spectator. You can even pretend to be puzzled that he will not accept the fact that the knot is genuine.

Have him pull on the ends of the rope. The knot will transform itself into an overhand knot right before his eyes.

If asked to perform this version of the Hunter knot in an impromptu setting where you do not have a chance to set up the convertible knot beforehand, there is a handling that is almost as good.

Bring the unprepared rope to the situation shown in Figure 310. Then take both ends of the rope in the left hand. Give the rope to the spectator. He may think you have formed nothing more than a slip knot in the rope. But when he pulls the ends of the rope, the knot will not dissolve. A complex, though genuine, knot has indeed formed in the rope.

Ropes That Think

The tricks in this chapter deal with mindreading and the supernatural. They are capable of being routined together to form a short act based on telepathy and the paranormal.

52. Liar's Ropes

The magician displays two ropes as shown in Figure 313. The ropes are equal in length. One rope has a knot in the bottom. A spectator is asked to choose silently either the rope with the knot or the other rope.

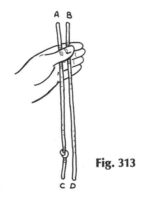

Fig. 313

The magician asks the spectator two questions. He explains that the spectator is to lie deliberately and answer yes to each question. The magician asks, "Did you choose the rope with the knot?" The spectator answers yes. Then the magician asks, "Did you choose the rope without the knot?" The spectator says yes again.

"The ropes are like Pinocchio's nose," the magician says. "One of them stretches when you tell a lie."

The spectator is asked to name truthfully the rope he chose. Say he names the knotted rope. The other rope is placed aside. Then the knotted rope visibly stretches so it is half again as long as it was originally.

There are no gimmicks.

Method: Two lengths of rope are used. One is 36″ long. The other is 54″ long. Tie a knot near the end of the long piece. Loop the short length around the middle of the long piece, Figure 314. Then tie a knot in the ropes at the point where the ropes loop over one another. Finally, tie another knot at the same distance up from the bottom ends *C–D*. When completed, the prepared ropes look as shown in Figure 315. It appears as if you have two ropes of equal length.

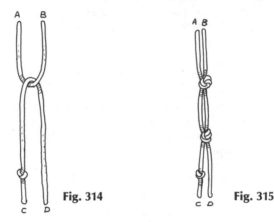

Fig. 314   Fig. 315

The prepared ropes may be carried in the pocket. When ready to perform, untie the lower knot. Then untie the upper knot but be sure that the looped centers of the ropes are concealed in the left palm when the upper knot is untied. Display the ropes as shown in Figure 313.

The right hand gathers ends *C* and *D* in the right palm. Then it gathers ends *A* and *B* in the right palm. The situation is shown in Figure 316. The left hand is shown open so the position of the looped centers is clear. In performance the left fingers would be closed around the rope.

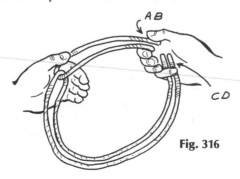

Fig. 316

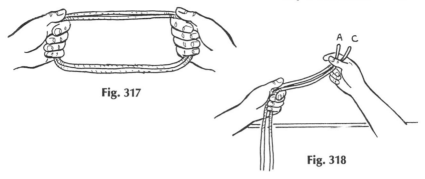

Fig. 317

Fig. 318

Stretch the rope between the hands as shown in Figure 317. It appears as if you have two pieces of rope of equal length. Then lower the left hand so it is below the level of the tabletop. Release the portion of the rope held by the left hand. The left hand then takes upper strand B and lower strand D and lowers them into the lap. The right hand holds ends A and C.

The left fingers curl around the two strands of rope and rest near the edge of the table. The situation is shown in Figure 318. Remark that the ropes are equal in length. Have the spectator choose either the rope with the knot or the other rope. Ask him if he chose the rope with the knot, instructing him to answer yes. Then ask if he chose the other rope, again instructing him to answer yes. Clearly, he has lied in answer to one question.

Have the spectator tell you which rope he really chose, explaining that the ropes act as a lie detector. Say he chose the knotted rope. Draw the two strands about 8″ to the right. Pause, drop the two strands A–B and C–D on the table and then grasp the strands nearer the left hand. The right hand then draws the two strands farther to the right, pulling the ropes from the left hand in a smooth action until another 8″ strand has been drawn to the right. Continue the process until end B comes into view, Figure 319.

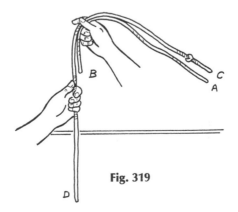

Fig. 319

Say, "Since you told a lie, the knotted rope, the one you chose, will stretch. This is sometimes called stretching the truth." The right hand draws C–D out a bit from the left hand, then a bit more, then draws it all the way out. The result is that rope C–D appears to stretch 18″.

If he chose the unknotted rope, say, "There's a saying that if you give a man enough rope, he'll hang himself. This should be enough rope." Draw C–D out as described above.

In either case, the audience sees one rope stretch 18″. At the finish, both ropes may be left with the audience. This routine is based on an idea of U. F. Grant.

53.   Thought Knots

The magician writes a prediction and places it in full view. He hands out short lengths of rope to each of five spectators. Each spectator ties a few knots in his rope. The ropes are gathered and the total number of knots counted. Say there are 15 knots.

Any spectator opens *Self-Working Rope Magic* to the first page of any chapter and counts to the fifteenth word. The word is "of." The prediction is opened. It correctly states that "of" would be chosen.

Method: The number of knots must total 15. To do this in a simple way, arrange it so one spectator is a confederate. Hand out short lengths of rope to each of five spectators. The confederate is the last spectator to get a rope.

Have each spectator tie a few knots in his rope. As you gather the ropes, count aloud how many knots have been tied. The confederate hears the running total and knows how many more knots to add to bring the total to 15. He ties this many knots in his rope.

Have another spectator check the total. Then have him open this book to the first page of any chapter. He can even open to the introduction. He counts to the fifteenth word. The book has been rigged to force the word "of," so your prediction will be correct if you wrote "of" as the prediction.

Since each spectator gets a short length of rope, he cannot tie more than three or four knots. This helps insure that the total will not go over 15. If the total number of knots in the first four ropes is 15, the confederate ties no knots. If the total exceeds 15, hand the fourth rope to the confederate and invite him to untie as many knots as he likes. He unties enough knots to bring the total down to 15. This covers all possibilities.

Self-Working Rope Magic was arranged as a force book by Sam Schwartz.

54.   Wishing Rings

The magician remarks that, while shopping in a store that specialized in antiques, he found a box that contained an assortment of strange-looking rings and ropes. The owner explained that one ring possessed a power. If you correctly guessed which ring had the power, your wishes would come true.

As the magician patters, two rings are threaded onto two lengths of rope. The spectator chooses one ring. Instantly that ring drops free of the rope.

There are no gimmicks. All articles may be borrowed.

Method: Each of the two ropes should measure 36″ in length. Use plastic bracelets about 3″ in diameter or larger. The rings should be different colors, say green and red. All of the apparatus is carried in a cardboard box. The box is part of the trick. The following handling is based on a trick of U. F. Grant's.

Explain that, while in an antique shop, you saw a box that contained an odd assortment of rings and ropes. As you speak, open the box, remove the two rings and two ropes, then pass them around so the audience can see they are ordinary.

Take back the ropes and hold them as in Figure 320. Two ends are held between the right thumb and first finger. The other end of rope *A–B* is clipped at the base of the thumb and first finger. The other end of rope *C–D* is held between the left first and second fingers.

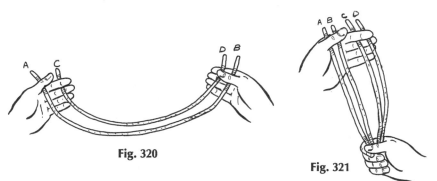

Fig. 320

Fig. 321

The right hand places end *B* between the left thumb and first finger. It then places end *D* between the left first and second fingers. The right hand then grasps the centers of the ropes. The situation is shown in Figure 321.

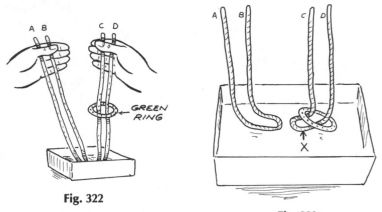

Fig. 322

Fig. 323

Place the centers of the two ropes into the cardboard box. Take back one ring, say the green ring, and hook it over ends C and D. The right hand then takes ends C and D, allowing the green ring to fall into the box, Figure 322.

The audience sees the green ring slide down onto the centers of the two ropes. The true situation is shown in the exposed view of Figure 323. The center of rope C–D is indicated by an X in this illustration for later reference.

The right hand now places end C into the left hand so it lies between the thumb and first finger next to end B. This is indicated in Figure 324. The right hand then deposits end D between the left first and second fingers as shown in Figure 325.

Take the red ring from the spectator. Drop it down over ends B and C as shown in Figure 326. Then grasp ends B and C with the right hand and allow the red ring to slide down into the cardboard box.

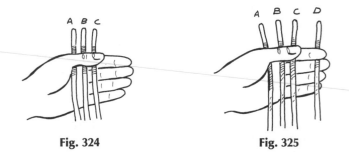

Fig. 324   **Fig. 325**

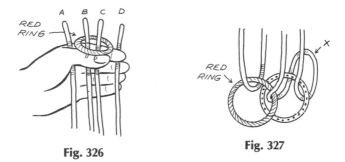

Fig. 326

Fig. 327

The situation now is that the red ring is genuinely linked onto the ropes but the green ring is not. Grasp all four ends with the left hand. Reach down into the box and hook the right little finger onto loop X shown in Figure 327. This will keep the green ring from falling off the rope. Then raise the hands as indicated in Figure 328. It appears as if both rings are securely linked onto the ropes.

The patter is to the effect that when you examined the contents of the box, the owner of the antique shop explained that the rings were wishing rings. If you guessed correctly, the ring with the power would grant a wish.

Ask the spectator to name a color. If he names red, say, "Does the red ring have the power?" As you speak, raise the ends of the ropes with the left hand. At the same time release the right hand's grip on the ropes. Look at the red ring as you do this. The red ring will remain on the rope but the green ring will fall off, Figure 329. Congratulate the spectator on having guessed correctly.

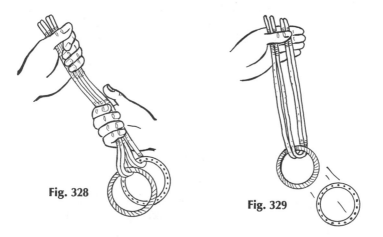

Fig. 328

Fig. 329

If the spectator names green, say, "Does the green ring have the power?" Whisk the ropes away, at the same time releasing the grip of the right little finger. Allow the green ring to remain in the right hand. Hold it aloft as you congratulate the spectator.

If borrowed articles are used, try to get a watch and a bracelet. The bracelet substitutes for the green ring, the watch for the red ring. Remark that you once played a game in which a correct guess would win a valuable prize. Have the spectator name either article. Then use the ambiguous wording described above to show that he made the correct guess. In this case, the bracelet will fall free of the ropes, the watch will remain in place.

55. Spirit Knots

The magician drops an ordinary piece of rope into a paper bag along with a finger ring. He shakes up the contents of the bag, explaining that a spirit inside the bag will tie three knots on the rope. He will also cause the ring to be tied on one of the knots.

The spectator is asked if he wants the ring to end up on the first knot, the second knot or the third knot.

Say the spectator chooses the second knot. The rope is removed from the bag. It has three knots in it and the ring is genuinely tied to the second knot!

Method: Two ropes are used. Each is about 48″ long. Two duplicate rings are also required. They can be inexpensive plastic rings obtainable in department stores.

One rope is prepared. Tie one of the rings to the center of the rope with a genuine overhand knot (No. 1). Then tie two slip knots (No. 8) on either side of the ring at intervals along the rope. The prepared rope is shown in Figure 330. The knot around the ring is the only genuine knot. The others are slip knots.

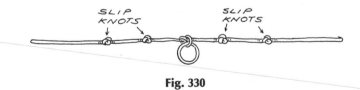

Fig. 330

Thread this rope up the right jacket sleeve so that one end protrudes into the palm. Drop the duplicate rope and ring into the paper bag.

When presenting the routine, remove the unprepared rope from the paper bag. Have the spectator tug on it to prove that it is a solid piece of rope. Then have him reach into the bag and remove the ring.

As attention focuses on the bag, hold the unprepared rope in the right hand so the end is in the right palm. Pull the end of the prepared rope up so it is clipped between the right thumb and first finger, Figure 331.

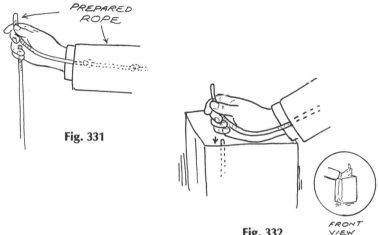

PREPARED
ROPE

Fig. 331

Fig. 332

FRONT
VIEW

Tell the spectator to drop the ring into the bag. Lower the rope into the bag until the base of the right hand is inside the bag, Figure 332. At this point, the unprepared rope is released so it falls silently into the bag.

Say, "There's a spirit inside the bag that can tie knots in the rope. To make it more difficult for him, I'll have him tie the ring onto one of the knots."

Have the spectator choose which knot he wants the ring to end up on. Say, "Do you want the ring in the first knot I pull from the bag, the second knot or the third knot?"

Assume the spectator chooses the second knot. Still keeping the right hand in place, with the left hand begin drawing the rope up into view. Although the rope comes from the sleeve, it appears to come from inside the paper bag.

At this point, the ring is knotted on the third knot. You want to lose one of the slip knots. It is done as follows. As the left hand pulls the rope upward, the first slip knot will enter the right palm.

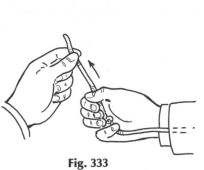

Fig. 333

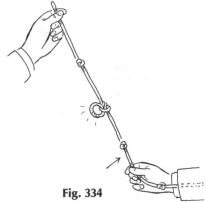

Fig. 334

When it does, curl the right little finger around the rope at a point just below the slip knot, Figure 333.

Hold the rope firmly in place with the little finger as the left hand continues to pull the rope upward. The result is that this slip knot will dissolve.

Continue pulling the rope with the left hand. Allow the next slip knot to be pulled into view. Allow the next knot to come into view. This is the genuine knot with the ring knotted to it.

Allow the next knot to come into view. At this point there are three knots visible to the audience, Figure 334. Release the left hand's grip on the rope and regrip the rope at a point below the third slip knot. This point is shown by the arrow in Figure 334.

The left hand continues to pull the rope upward. When the final slip knot is in the right palm, cause it to dissolve by the method illustrated in Figure 333.

To finish the routine, pretend to untie the slip knots. Go through the motions but really pull them so they dissolve. You will be left with the ring genuinely knotted to the rope. The rope can be tossed to the spectator for examination.

If the spectator said he wanted the ring to appear on the first knot, when you begin pulling the rope through the hand in Figure 333, dissolve the first and second slip knots. Then pull the rest of the rope into view.

If the spectator said he wanted the ring to appear on the third knot, pull the first three knots into view, then dissolve the last two slip knots.

Handled this way, the knots always appear evenly spaced on the rope at the finish.

56. Séance

The ends of an ordinary piece of rope are securely knotted together. The magician then causes several borrowed rings to teleport onto the rope. All may be left with the audience at the finish.

Fig. 335

Method: Required are two pieces of rope as shown in Figure 335, and a sheet of newspaper. To present the routine, hold the ropes as indicated in figure 336-A. You are going to tie a false knot like the one described in the Victor Rope Trick (No. 46). To summarize the handling, place end *A* over end *C*, Figure 336-B. Then twist end *C* down into the right palm, Figure 337-A. The left second finger kicks end *B* up into view, Figure 337-B. Tie *A* and *B* together around the long rope, pulling the knot snug. Then slide

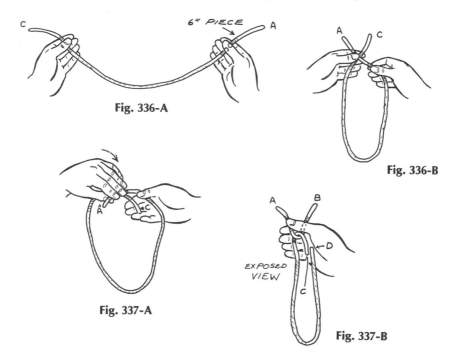

Fig. 336-A

Fig. 336-B

Fig. 337-A

Fig. 337-B

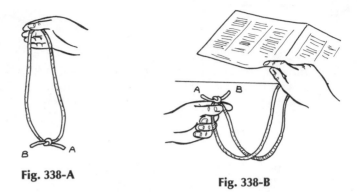

Fig. 338-A

Fig. 338-B

the knot down to the center of the rope as shown in Figure 338-A. Ends *C* and *D* are concealed in the right hand.

Without letting go of the ends of the rope, lift the newspaper with the right hand and place the knotted ends under the newspaper, Figure 338-B. The right hand then places ends *C* and *D* in the lap.

As the knot is made, ask two people to remove their finger rings. If one of the spectators wears no ring, ask if someone has a solid bracelet you can borrow. By the time the borrowed articles are collected, you have tied the knot in the rope and placed the knotted ends under the newspaper. The audience assumes the center of the rope is in the lap. The true situation, visible only from where you sit, is shown in Figure 339-A.

Remove your own finger ring and add it to the borrowed rings. Take one of the borrowed rings and place it below the level of the tabletop. As soon as it is out of sight, thread it onto the rope, then tie ends *C* and *D* together, Figure 339-B.

Remark that you will try to cause the ring to materialize onto the rope. Gather the knotted ends (*C* and *D*) and the ring into the right fist. Lift the newspaper with the left hand. Place the knotted ends plus the rings under the newspaper. Do not show the audience that the ring is on the rope.

Fig. 339-A   **Fig. 339-B**

Say that you will try the same feat with the other borrowed ring. Take this ring and place it out of sight below the level of the tabletop with the right hand. The left hand then reaches under the newspaper, takes ends *A* and *B*, conceals them in the fist and takes them into the lap.

The spectator sitting across from you may suspect that you are simply taking the knotted ends into the lap, untying them and threading the rings onto the rope. To do away with this suspicion, say to him, "Place your hand down flat on the newspaper, directly over the knotted ends of the rope." When he does this, he can feel the knotted ends through the newspaper. These are in fact the genuinely knotted ends *C* and *D*, so all is as it should be.

When ends *A* and *B* are in the lap, untie them. Thread the borrowed ring onto the short piece of rope, then hold this piece so that ends *A* and *B* are in the fist. Bring this segment into view. The situation is shown in the exposed view of Figure 340-A. The audience sees the view of Figure 340-B. It appears as if the borrowed ring is actually on the rope.

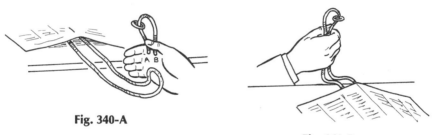

Fig. 340-A

Fig. 340-B

Lower the hand below the level of the tabletop. Remove the borrowed ring. Remark that you will dematerialize the ring to get it off. Pause for a moment, then toss the borrowed ring onto the table.

Take your own ring and place it below the level of the tabletop. Pretend to have trouble getting it onto the rope. Say, "Mine is the only ring that won't cooperate." Secretly gather the short piece of rope *A–B* into the hand. Hold your ring at the fingertips and place it in your pocket, along with rope *A–B*. This gets rid of the extra piece of rope.

Say, "Two rings out of three is pretty good." To this point the audience has not actually seen that the first borrowed ring materialized onto the rope. Have the spectator reach under the newspaper and withdraw the rope. He does, and discovers that one of the rings is securely linked onto the rope.

57. The Hanging

This is a strange detective story in which several spectators are invited to assist. At the magician's request, each draws a card from the deck. The spectator holding the ♠A plays the part of the guilty party. His identity is unknown to anyone except himself.

While the cards are being drawn, the magician fashions a noose out of a length of rope. The patter is to the effect that the guilty party will give himself away when he handles the rope.

The rope is given to the first spectator. He is asked to pull the ends with as much force as he likes. If he is guilty, the noose will tighten. Otherwise it will remain fast, no matter how hard he pulls on the ends of the rope.

The rope is passed from one spectator to the next. In each case the noose remains unchanged. But when the rope is pulled by the guilty party, the noose mysteriously tightens. Nothing more is required than a piece of rope and a pack of cards. This fine trick was invented by Robert E. Neale.

Method: The person who draws the ♠A must be known to the magician. An easy way to accomplish this without anyone knowing is to secretly mark the back of the ♠A with a pencil. Have the deck thoroughly shuffled. Ask someone to remove the cards comprising a royal flush in spades (♠A, ♠K, ♠Q, ♠J, ♠10), mix them face down and deal them face down on the table. Have each of five people draw a card. Simply note which person gets the pencil-marked ♠A.

The noose is fashioned out of the rope using an odd form of a slip knot that remains under the magician's control at all times.

Begin with a 60″ length of rope and hold it as shown in Figure 341. The right hand then moves to the position shown in Figure 342. The rope is draped over the left wrist and brought to the position of Figure 343. This is the opening phase of the Hunter knot (No. 47) but from here the handling differs.

The left hand grips its end between thumb and first finger. The left third and fourth fingers then move down behind the rope in

Fig. 341

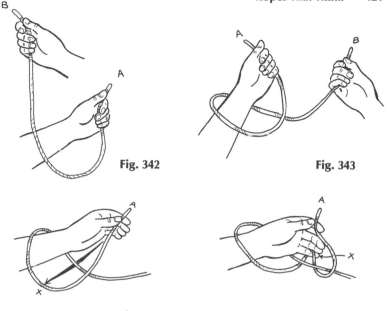

Fig. 342   **Fig. 343**

Fig. 344   **Fig. 345**

the direction of the arrows shown in Figure 344. They grip the rope at the point marked *X*. Then they straighten to the position shown in Figure 345.

Allow the portion of the rope that is over the left wrist to slip off the back of the hand. The right hand then draws its end away, causing the rope to tighten and form two loops as shown in Figure 346. Make sure the left third and fourth fingers retain their grip on the rope until the knot has been pulled snug.

Once the two loops have been formed, release the grip on the left third and fourth fingers. Then pull the ends of the rope away from one another. The lower loop in Figure 346 will close. There will be a single loop in the rope.

Apparently you have done nothing more than tie a noose in the

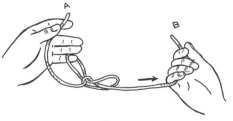

Fig. 346

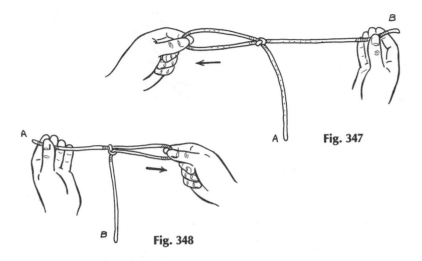

Fig. 347

Fig. 348

rope, but this is a special noose, for no matter how hard the spectator pulls the ends, the noose will not tighten.

You can tug on the noose by pulling it to the left, Figure 347. The noose will not tighten. But if you pull the noose to the right, as shown in Figure 348, the knot is converted to a slip knot. Now the noose will tighten when the ends of the rope are pulled.

To present the trick, fashion the noose while the cards are being chosen as described above. Remember which spectator gets the ♠ A. Hand the rope to the first spectator. Tug on the noose by pulling it to the left as shown in Figure 347. This emphasizes how snug the noose is. Have the spectator pull the ends of the rope. The noose does not tighten.

Repeat the same procedure with each spectator in turn. When you get to the spectator who holds the ♠ A, tug on the noose but this time tug it to the right as shown in Figure 348, so that the slip knot is formed. When the spectator pulls the ends of the rope, the knot will tighten.

The trick can be done in such a way that you do not need to know the guilty party. Further, once the rope is handed to the first spectator, you never touch it again. The secret is to work with a confederate who spots which spectator gets the pencil-marked ♠ A. He then endeavors to stand to the right of this party. Have the spectators stand in a line. Give the rope to the first spectator. He tugs on the rope and gives it to the next man in line. When the confederate has tugged on the rope, he converts it to a slip knot before passing it on to the guilty party. When the guilty man gets the rope, the noose mysteriously tightens.

Miracle Move

Jack Miller was a magic innovator. In the 1920s he began experimenting with ways of causing a ring to appear as if it were genuinely linked onto a rope. When some of his methods were released in 1945, they were immediately put to use by magicians looking for strong visual material.

This chapter describes the basic routine plus two variations. The visual illusion produced by Miller's approach can be exploited in a variety of ways to produce strong magical effects.

58. Miller's Move

The ends of a rope are tied together with a genuine knot. An ungimmicked ring is tossed onto the table or floor. The magician lowers the loop of rope onto the ring in the same way one would lower a fishing pole into the water to catch a fish. In this instance the magician catches the ring onto the rope. The ring is genuinely linked on the rope. The ends of the rope have to be untied in order to get the ring off.

Method: Use a piece of rope about 36″ in length. The ring should be of a size to fit easily over the arm. A ring 10″ in diameter would be large enough for this purpose.

Stand with the right side to the audience. Thread one end of the rope through the ring as shown in Figure 349. The left hand brings the ring up to a point about 6″ from the top of the rope. The right fingers then curl inward, clipping the rope between the right third and fourth fingers as shown in Figure 350.

Fig. 349

Fig. 350

Fig. 351

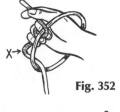

Fig. 352

Fig. 353

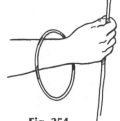

Fig. 354

The ring was brought up in Figure 350 to flip it up over onto the right arm in the following way. The left hand raises the ring to the position shown in Figure 351. Then it allows the ring to flip over to the position shown in Figure 352. At this point the ring is technically off the rope, but it appears to be still threaded onto the rope because of the small loop clipped between the right third and fourth fingers. This small loop is concealed from the audience. The audience sees the back of the right hand at this point.

Grasp the rope with the left hand at a point just below the right fourth finger. This point is indicated by the arrow in Figure 352. Pull this strand of rope out of the ring. The result is shown in Figure 353. From the audience's view, the situation looks as shown in Figure 354. The rope appears to be free of the ring.

Tie the ends of the rope together. Then pull the ring back a few inches toward the elbow. This lengthens the loop around the ring. The situation is indicated in Figure 355. Remember that the back of the right hand is toward the audience. The right arm hides the loop from the audience's view. At this point the audience sees the situation as shown in Figure 356. The illusion that the ring is free from the rope is perfect.

Hold the rope with the left hand. At the same time drop both hands. The ring falls to the table. The rope falls on top of it in a tangled condition like that shown in Figure 357. Lower the rope. Then lift the rope, holding it in both hands to form the triangle shown in Figure 358. You have caught the ring on the center of the rope. The rope must be untied to get the ring off.

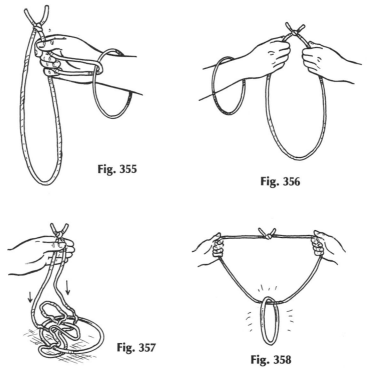

Fig. 355

Fig. 356

Fig. 357

Fig. 358

59. Hummering I

Working independently of Jack Miller, Bob Hummer devised a curious variation of the basic principle. While the spectator holds one end of the rope and the magician the other, an ungimmicked ring is threaded onto the rope.

Method: Thread a rope through a ring or bracelet as shown in Figure 359. Grasp end *A* with the left hand. Have the spectator grasp end *B*. Drape a handkerchief over the apparatus so the ring is hidden from the spectator's view.

Fig. 359

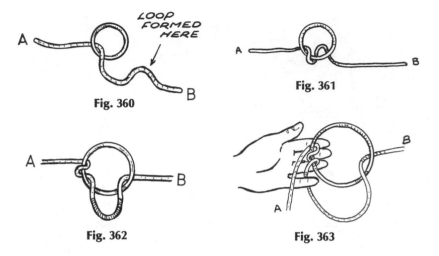

Fig. 360

Fig. 361

Fig. 362

Fig. 363

Reach under the handkerchief and form a loop as shown in Figure 360. Bring it around behind the ring as shown in Figure 361. Then pull it through the ring as shown in Figure 362. Grasp the loop between the left third and fourth fingers as indicated in Figure 363. Close the other fingers and thumb around the rope and ring to conceal the extra rope looped around the ring.

Remove the handkerchief. The situation appears as shown in Figure 364. The ring is still threaded on the rope. Say, "I was going to try to remove the ring from the rope, but that can be done only by letting go of one end."

Take end B from the spectator and thread it through the ring in the direction shown by the arrow in Figure 365. The ring appears to be free of the rope. Hand end B back to the spectator. Say, "But it's easy to get the ring onto the rope while the ends are held."

Replace the handkerchief over the ring. Reach under the handkerchief and pretend to make an adjustment. Then remove the handkerchief. The rope is now looped around the ring twice.

Fig. 364

Fig. 365

60.   Hummering II

In an equally curious version of Hummering, the handling is the same through Figure 364. This time, thread end *B* through in the direction of the arrow in Figure 366, as if to secure the rope around the ring with a double strand. Cover the apparatus with a handkerchief. This time reach under the handkerchief with the right hand and completely remove the ring from the rope. Say, "It was easier than I thought."

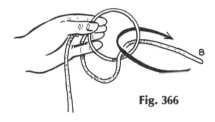

Fig. 366

61.   Releaso

A ring is fairly threaded onto a long piece of rope. The ends of the rope are tied. The ring is clearly seen to be looped onto the rope, yet it instantly releases itself.

Method: This clever routine is based on ideas of Jack Miller and Peter Warlock. Use a ring about 10″ in diameter and a rope about 5′ long. Stand so the back of the right hand is toward the audience. Thread the ring onto the rope as shown in Figure 367.

Curl the right second, third and fourth fingers around the rope as shown in Figure 368. The back of the right hand is toward the audience.

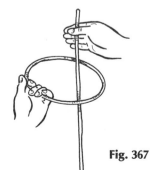 

Fig. 367   **Fig. 368**

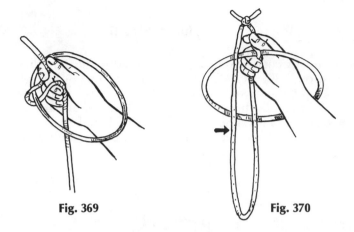

Fig. 369   **Fig. 370**

The left hand places the ring over onto the right arm, Figure 369. The apparent reason for doing this is so that the left hand will be free to aid in knotting the ends of the rope. In reality the ring is already off the rope at this point.

The ends of the rope are now tied together, Figure 370. Grasp the strand indicated by the arrow in Figure 370 and bring it around to the other side of the ring. This brings you to the position shown in Figure 371. The audience's view is shown in Figure 372. It appears as if the ring is fairly threaded onto the rope.

Grasp the two strands of the rope with the left first and second fingers, Figure 373. Pull them to the left. Then release the right hand's grip on the rope, allowing the ring to hang as shown in

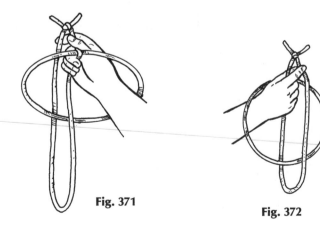

Fig. 371

Fig. 372

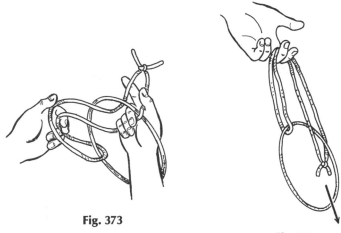

Fig. 373

Fig. 374

Figure 374. Again it appears as if the ring is genuinely linked to the rope.

Grasp the knotted ends with the right hand and pull them downward in the direction shown by the arrow in Figure 374. The ring will rise up to the left hand. Grasp the ring with the left hand and turn the left hand palm up so the ring rests on the left palm. At the same time, continue pulling on the rope with the right hand.

The rope will free itself from the ring, resulting in the release shown in Figure 375.

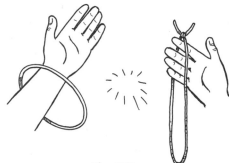

Fig. 375

Psychic Rope Ties

In the middle of the nineteenth century, spiritualists gained popularity with séances where phenomena of a spooky nature transpired. The spirit medium was tied to a chair. The room was darkened. Immediately, denizens of the spirit world brought about levitations, teleportations and other spirit manifestations.

Since the spirit medium was securely tied to the chair, he was incapable of secretly performing the spiritualist feats. The audience at these sittings could only conclude that beings from another world, summoned by the medium, were responsible for the strange phenomena they witnessed.

This chapter deals with psychic feats of a similar nature. It is difficult to darken a room completely, so a different setting will be used in the following tricks.

In these tricks, the magician is securely tied and left alone in a room. The door is closed. While alone, the magician endeavors to summon spirit forces. When the assembled guests return to the room, they find that the spirits did leave behind some sign of their presence. The magician is still securely tied.

62. Telekinetic Ring

The end of a piece of rope is tied around the magician's left wrist. The other end is threaded through the keyhole in the door. It is held by a spectator on the other side of the door.

The magician borrows a ring from a spectator. Stepping behind the door for a moment, he summons a ghost from the spirit world, who causes the ring to teleport onto the rope.

Method: After one end of the rope has been tied to the left wrist, have the other end threaded through the keyhole, Figure 376. When the spectators have left the room, place the borrowed ring against the center of the rope. Bring a loop of rope up through the ring as shown in Figure 377.

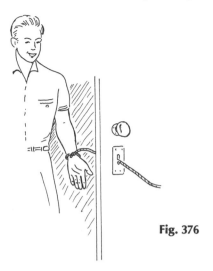

Fig. 376

Feed the loop through the rope that circles the left wrist, Figure 378. Then bring the loop over the left hand, Figure 379. Feed it through the rope that circles the left hand as indicated in Figure 380. Finally, bring the loop up in the direction shown by the arrow in Figure 380 and over the left hand again.

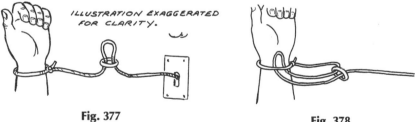

Fig. 377

Fig. 378

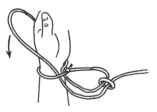

Fig. 379 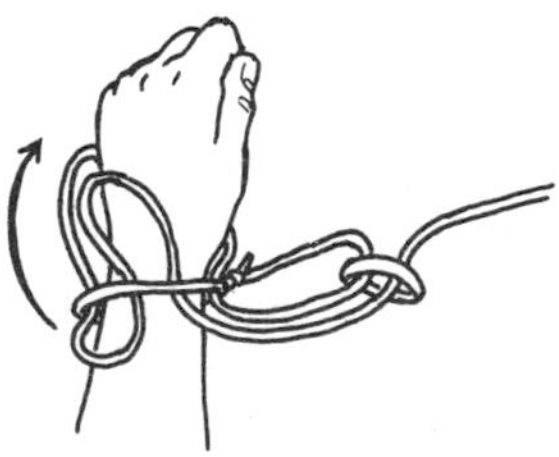   **Fig. 380**

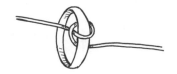

Fig. 381

A knot will have formed in the rope. Work it over the ring. The result is that the ring is now knotted onto the rope as shown in Figure 381.

Objects other than rings may be used. If you use a plastic bracelet of your own, it is possible for the bracelet to become linked to the rope in an instant.

Buy two identical bracelets of a size large enough to fit over the arm. Slide one onto the wrist and under the shirt sleeve just before the performance.

When you are ready to perform, have the wrist tied and the other end of the rope fed through the keyhole. Ask the spectator to initial a plastic ring. This is the duplicate of the ring in the sleeve.

Step behind the door. Grasp the ring in the sleeve and slide it down the rope. Immediately step into view, showing the ring on the rope. Say you will try something harder. Step back out of view. Slide the ring back inside the sleeve so it is hidden. Then knot the signed ring onto the rope by the method shown in Figures 377–381. Step back into view again and have the spectator verify the initials.

When doing the above trick or any of the tricks in this chapter, you can have adhesive tape wrapped around the knots after the rope has been knotted to the wrist. The spectator can sign the tape. This does away with the suspicion that you untied the rope when you were out of the spectator's view.

63.   Fourth-Dimension Knot

The magician's wrists are securely tied with a length of rope. The knots may be sealed with tape. He enters another room for a moment, saying that he will pass the rope through the fourth dimension. When he returns, a genuine knot has been tied in the rope, as shown in Figure 382. There are no gimmicks.

Fig. 382

Method: Books describing this classic effect instruct the reader to form a loop in the rope and feed it through the portion circling one of the wrists, but most do not make it clear exactly how this is done. If the loop is incorrectly made, no knot will form.

To form the knot, first have the wrists tied with a 36″ length of rope. Make sure the portion circling each wrist is snug but not tight. The knots may be sealed with tape.

Explain that you know a fourth-dimension spirit who ties knots in rope. Step behind a door. When you are out of sight, bring a portion of rope up through the strand circling the left wrist, Figure 383. Then form a loop by twisting the rope from left to right, Figure 384. Maintaining the twist in the rope, bring the loop up in the direction shown by the arrow in Figure 384.

Slip the loop over the fingertips, Figure 385. Turn the left hand palm down. Then slide the loop in the direction shown by the arrow in Figure 386, working it under the strand around the wrist.

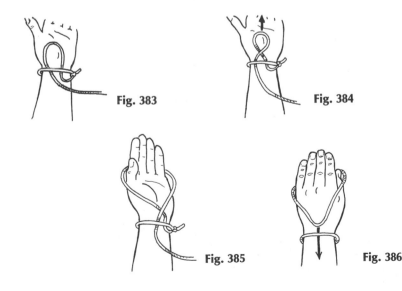

Fig. 383

Fig. 384

Fig. 385

Fig. 386

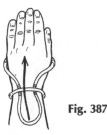

Fig. 387

This brings you to the situation pictured in Figure 387. Bring the loop over the strand circling the wrist, in the direction shown by the arrow in Figure 387. Then bring it back over the left hand. You will have formed an overhand knot in the rope. Bring the knot to the center of the rope. The result is shown in Figure 382. Step back from behind the door to display the knot.

Remember to twist the rope from left to right, as shown in Figure 384. If you twist it from right to left, no knot will form, though if you twist it twice from right to left you will get an overhand knot.

With a slight addition to this method, you can perform a startling impromptu trick. After the wrists are bound, you step behind a door. When you step back, an overhand knot has formed in the rope. Expressing disappointment that the spirit accomplished relatively little, you step behind the door, then *immediately* step back into view. Now there is a second knot in the rope and it is a figure 8.

The method is almost the same. When you first step behind the door, draw up the strand as shown in Figure 383, then give the rope a twist from left to right. Give it another twist from left to right. The doubly twisted loop is then brought over the hand as shown in Figures 385–387. The result is that a figure-8 knot is formed in the rope.

Work this knot over toward the left wrist so that it blends in with the knot that already binds this wrist. When you have done this, form a conventional knot by the method shown in Figures 383–387. Bring this knot to the center of the rope.

Step out into view. Explain that the spirit tied a knot in the rope. Display the knot. Allow a spectator to examine the knot to verify that it is genuine. Then say that the spirit, having warmed up, might want to attempt something more ambitious.

Step behind the door. Draw the figure 8 away from the wrist so it too is at the center of the rope. Immediately step back into view. Now there are two entirely different knots on the rope.

The Fourth-Dimension Knot makes a good follow-up to the Hunter knot (No. 47). First form the Hunter knot. Repeat it one or two times. Then offer to make the conditions more strict. Have the rope tied to your wrists. Here manipulation is clearly out of the question. Turn your back or place the hands out of sight below the table. Perform the above method to show that a knot has formed in the rope under impossible conditions.

64.   Locked in Place

A blank piece of paper is signed by the spectator. It is placed in an envelope and taped to the wall in the dining room. The magician has his wrists securely tied. The knots may be sealed with adhesive tape. A length of ribbon is looped around the wrists, Figure 388, and threaded through the keyhole in the door leading from the dining room to the living room.

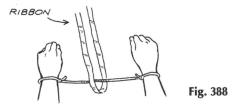

Fig. 388

The ribbon is pulled snug so that the magician must stand near the door. He is thus 10′–12′ from the envelope taped to the wall.

The spectators leave the dining room and close the door. One spectator standing outside the door holds the ribbon secure. A minute later, when the spectators open the door and return to the dining room, the magician is still securely tied in place, yet the signed paper has been torn in half.

Method: Have the hands tied as shown in Figure 388. Have a length of ribbon looped over the rope and threaded through the keyhole as shown in Figure 389. Explain that the reason for using ribbon is to make it easier to thread the strands through the keyhole. Actually, the reason is to make the following manipulation easier.

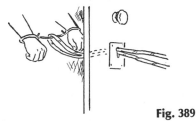

Fig. 389

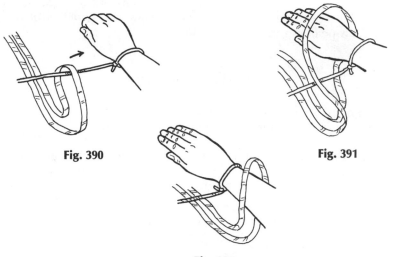

Fig. 390   **Fig. 391**

Fig. 392

When you are alone in the room, slide the ribbon toward the palm-down right wrist as shown in Figure 390. Bring it over the right hand, Figure 391, to a position behind the rope encircling the right wrist, Figure 392.

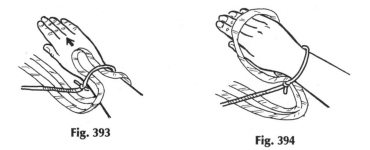

Fig. 393

Fig. 394

Slip the ribbon under the rope encircling the wrist, Figure 393, then forward and over the right fingertips, Figure 394. A view from below at this point is shown in Figure 395. When the ribbon is brought over the fingertips, slip it through the rope encircling the wrist as shown in Figure 396. The ribbon is now free from the rope.

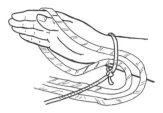

Fig. 395

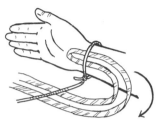

Fig. 396

Loop the ribbon twice around the doorknob. This is just a precaution. If the spectator on the other side of the door tugs on the ribbon, he will feel tension on the ribbon.

Walk quietly to the envelope taped to the wall, remove the paper, quietly tear it in half and return the torn paper to the envelope. Then return to the door. By reversing the moves shown in Figures 390–396 you will get the ribbon back onto the rope.

When the spectators return to the room they will find you securely tied. On examining the envelope they will discover that the paper has been torn.

When you are free of the ribbon, you can set up other tests. For example, since the dining room is usually adjacent to the kitchen, you can inflate a large red balloon and leave it in the dishwasher. Return to the dining room, tear the paper, then loop the ribbon back onto the rope.

Have the spectators enter and verify that the paper was torn while you were securely tied. Then have a spectator remove an uninflated red balloon from your pocket. Tell him to knot the end and return the balloon to your pocket. Have the spectators leave the room. You are still tied. Silently count to five. Remove the balloon and hide it in another pocket.

When the spectators return they find that the knotted balloon has somehow inflated itself and has been transported to the dishwasher in the kitchen.

If you have trouble threading the ribbon through the keyhole, it can be passed under the door and held by the spectator.

65.   Watch the Watch

A short length of rope is tied to each of the magician's wrists as shown in Figure 397. The magician crosses his arms. The ropes are tied together behind his back, Figure 398.

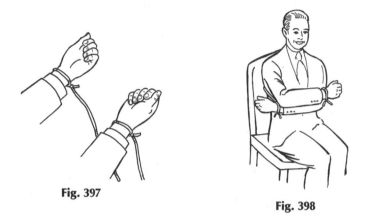

Fig. 397

Fig. 398

A spectator drops his watch into the magician's right jacket pocket. The spectators leave the room and close the door. A few seconds later they reenter the room. The borrowed watch is now on the magician's left ankle. On closer examination it is found that the watch has been set back several hours. The knots in the rope may be sealed by the spectators to prove they have not been tampered with.

Method: Use two pieces of rope, each about 36" in length. Have one tied around each wrist as in Figure 397. Cross the arms exactly as shown in figure 398. As you do, take a deep breath to expand the chest. The chest can be held in the expanded condition while breathing normally.

Have the ropes tied together behind the back. A spectator drops his watch into your right jacket pocket.

When the door has been closed and you are alone in the room, release all air from the lungs. With the chest no longer in an expanded condition you gain slack in the ropes. This is not strictly necessary but it makes the handling easier.

Shift the left hand as far as possible to the right. This too is to gain slack in the ropes. The right hand then slides upward as shown in Figure 399, and over the head. Quickly remove the watch

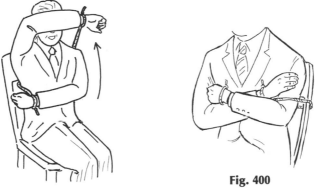

Fig. 400

Fig. 399

from the right pocket, set it back several hours and slip it onto the left ankle.

Bring the right hand back over the head and assume the seated position shown in Figure 398 again. The above moves can be done quickly. As soon as you are back in the original position, signal the spectators to come back into the room.

They see that you are still tied and that the knots have not been tampered with. The spectator looks for the watch in your right pocket. He discovers that it has been transported to your left ankle, and further that the hands have been set back several hours.

Another presentation is to tie a spectator and have him sit in the room with you. He is not tied as shown in Figure 398. Instead, have him tied as shown in Figure 400. The hands are crossed before being tied behind the back. It is a small but crucial difference. He cannot escape from this kind of tie without assistance.

You are then tied as shown in Figure 398. You both sit in the room, back to back. The lights are turned out and the door closed. In the darkness, bring the hands to the position shown in Figure 399, remove the watch, set the hands back, then drop the watch into the spectator's side pocket. Resume the position shown in Figure 398.

When the other spectators enter the room they find both of you securely tied, but now the borrowed watch is in the spectator's pocket.

66.   Gysel Spirit Tie

Robert Gysel devised one of the best spirit ties. Each wrist is tied with a piece of rope. The arms are crossed and the hands tied behind the back. Then the ends of the rope are tied to the chair in which the performer is seated. The knots may be sealed with tape or wax. The ropes may be marked by the spectators for later identification.

After the performer has been securely tied to the chair, a cup is placed on the table. Alongside it are placed a spoon, a napkin and a glass of water. This, the performer explains, is the place setting for a friendly ghost.

The spectators exit the room and close the door, leaving the performer alone. Immediately he asks them to return. When they do they find that the spoon is now inside the cup, the napkin has a knot in it and the glass, brimful with water a moment before, is now empty.

Method: Use two pieces of rope, each about 48″ in length. Have the end of one rope tied around the left wrist, the end of the other rope around the right wrist, Figure 401. Bring the hands together as shown in Figure 402.

As the hands cross one another, grasp the left rope in the right hand and the right rope in the left hand, Figure 403. Without hesitation, bring the hands across the chest as shown in Figure 404. An exposed view is shown in Figure 405.

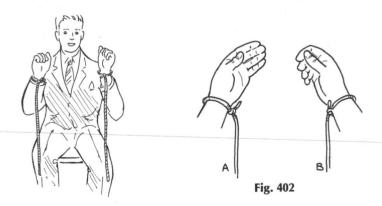

A   B

Fig. 402

Fig. 401

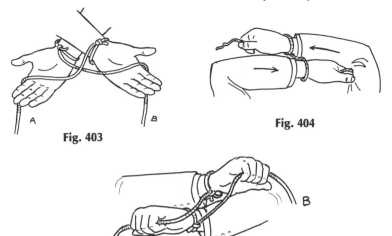

Fig. 403

Fig. 404

Fig. 405

When the hands reach the position shown in Figure 406, have the ropes tied behind the back. This is shown from the front in Figure 407. A side view is indicated in Figure 408. The ends of the ropes are then tied to the chair.

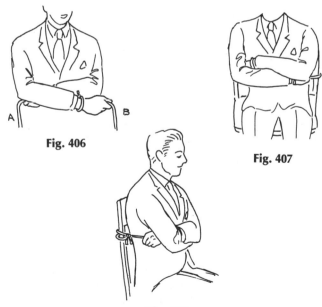

Fig. 406

Fig. 407

Fig. 408

Fig. 409

The above description is based on Tarbell's account of the Gysel tie. When completed, it appears as if you have been legitimately tied to the chair.

Have a glass of water, a cup and spoon, and a napkin placed on the table. When the spectators exit from the room and close the door, simply separate the arms, Figure 409. Drink the water, knot the napkin and place the spoon in the cup. Then cross the arms again and have the spectators reenter the room. You appear to be securely tied to the chair. The spirits have visited the room and left behind evidence of their visit. After you are untied, the entire apparatus may be left with the audience.

67.   Spirit Music

If you have access to an accordion, a remarkable test can be performed. As the audience sees it, the accordion is placed on a table. The magician is securely tied to a chair. When he is alone in the room and the door is closed, the accordion can be heard playing.

Spectators can return to the room immediately. The accordion is undisturbed on the table. The magician is still tied to the chair. The sound of the accordion can be heard right up to the instant the spectators open the door.

Method: This feat was used by nineteenth-century spiritualists. The Amazing Randi has suggested a remarkably simple way it can be done. The sound of an accordion can be almost duplicated by a harmonica.

Have the harmonica in the pocket. When you are tied to the chair by means of the Gysel tie and left alone in the room with the accordion, release yourself from the rope tie, remove the harmonica from the pocket and play a few notes. Then return the harmonica to the pocket and cross the arms so you appear to be tied to the chair.

68.   The Kellar Tie

Harry Kellar invented a rope tie that looks secure but allows you to release your hands quickly. With this tie you can perform amusing tricks like the following.

Two spectators tie the magician's hands together. The spectators remove their watches and place them on a table. One spectator takes back his watch. When the other reaches for his watch, he discovers it is gone. The watch is found on the magician's wrist, even though the magician's hands are still tied together.

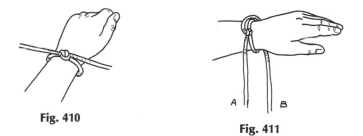

Fig. 410

Fig. 411

Method: This method is Harlan Tarbell's modified handling of the original Kellar rope tie. Use a piece of rope about 36″ in length.

Have a spectator stand on either side of you. Extend your left hand. Have a spectator tie the left wrist snugly to the center of the rope as shown in Figure 410.

Ask the spectator to release the rope. The ends fall as shown in Figure 411. Clip strand *B* between the left first and second fingers, Figure 412. Bring the left hand up to the position shown in Figure 413.

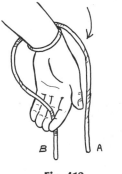

Fig. 412

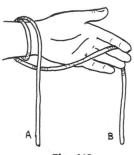

Fig. 413

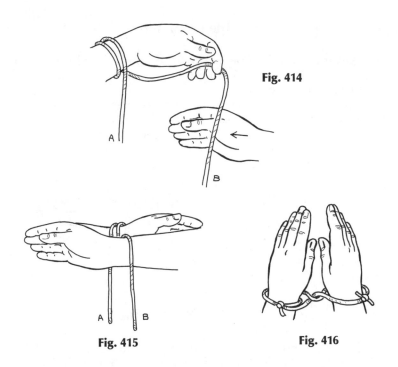

Fig. 414

Fig. 415   Fig. 416

Slip the right hand between strands *A* and *B* as shown in Figure 414. It should appear to the audience that you hold strand *B* up only to allow the right hand to move under this strand.

Hold the wrists against one another as shown in Figure 415. Have the spectators tie strands *A* and *B* together so that the wrists are securely tied. The result is shown in Figure 416.

Have the spectators stand alongside one another facing the audience. Step in back of them. There should be a table to the right. The situation is shown in Figure 417.

Ask each spectator to remove his watch. Have spectator One hand his watch to spectator Two. Then spectator Two places both watches on the table. Explain that you are going to cause the setting on one watch to change magically by one hour. To prevent sleight of hand, you have had your wrists tied.

As you speak, you have time to release your right hand. The release is done as follows. Beginning with the hands as in Figure 416, turn the left hand to the right and the right hand to the left to the position shown in Figure 418. Bring the right hand to the position shown in Figure 419. That hand can now be slipped free of the rope.

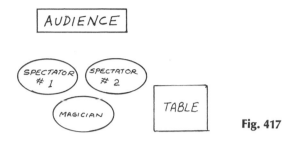

Fig. 417

Grasp the rope as shown in Figure 420. This keeps the loop open and makes it easy for the right hand to slip back into place later on.

Since you stand behind the spectators, the above release is done without anyone knowing that it is taking place. As you perform the secret release, ask spectator Two to pick up spectator One's watch and hand it back to him. Tell spectator One to check the setting. As soon as audience attention is focused on spectator One, reach to the table, take spectator Two's watch and slip it on the right wrist.

Put the right hand back into the loop being held by the left thumb and first finger. To cause the hands to appear to be securely tied, simply reverse the action, going from Figure 419 to Figure 418 and then to Figure 417.

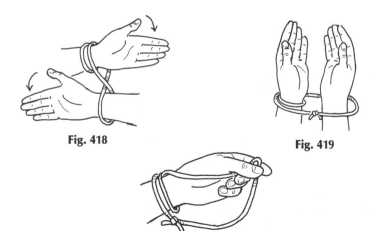

Fig. 418

Fig. 419

Fig. 420

The spectators announce that the setting on spectator One's watch did not change. Remark that you might have better luck with the other watch. When spectator Two exclaims that his watch is missing, step forward and say, "Well, you can have mine." Have your wrists untied. Then remove the watch and give it back to the spectator.

When you gain facility with the method, you may want to perform the tie as it is usually done on the stage. The tie is the same, but the hands are tied behind the back. This allows you to release the right hand behind the back while facing the spectator. You can then do a stunt like the following.

Have your hands tied together behind your back. Step behind the spectator. As you do, release the right hand. Then tap the spectator on the shoulder and quickly slip the right hand back into place. The spectator will be surprised, since he is positive he tied your hands tightly together. The audience will laugh at the startled look on the spectator's face.

69.   Six Glasses

Six glasses are placed on the table. Three are filled with liquid as shown in Figure 421. The spectator is told that by moving two adjacent glasses at a time he can end up so that filled and empty glasses alternate as in Figure 422.

A   B   C   D   E   F

Fig. 421

Fig. 422

The spectator tries and, eventually, succeeds. He will find it a time-consuming task to solve the puzzle.

The glasses are again put back to the position shown in Figure 421. The magician is tied. The spectators leave the room. The second they close the door they are asked to return to the room.

Fig. 423

The glasses now alternate as shown in Figure 422. The magician is still tied. He explains that a puzzle-solving ghost quickly did the puzzle.

Method: There are many ways of solving the puzzle by moving two adjacent glasses at a time. One is to move glasses *A* and *B* to the right of *F*, as shown in Figure 423. Then move *F* and *G* to the right of *H*. Finally, move *C* and *D* to positions *F* and *G*.

It takes time to solve the puzzle by the above method, especially if the glasses are brimful and another stipulation is that you cannot spill any liquid.

After you are tied with rope using the Kellar tie and are alone in the room, you can instantly solve the puzzle by releasing yourself from the tie, then pouring the contents of glass *B* into glass *E*. Immediately get yourself back into the tied position and call the spectators into the room. It is obvious to them that you could not possibly have had enough time to untie yourself, switch glasses around and retie yourself.

70.   Adam's Apple

This final rope tie should be reserved for occasions when circumstances are just right. It uses a method different from any covered thus far in this chapter.

The magician sits in a chair. His hands are securely tied to the arms of the chair. A spectator takes an apple from a bowl of fruit and places it in the magician's right hand.

The room lights are turned out and then turned on again. The apple is now seen in the magician's left hand. The magician rotates the apple in his left hand. A bite has been taken from the apple. He opens his mouth to show that the missing portion is in his mouth.

Method: This amusing trick was devised by Bruce Elliott. It uses a confederate. Before doing the trick, surreptitiously remove an apple from a bowl of fruit, take a bite from it and put the apple back. Keep the piece of apple in the mouth.

Have the hands tied to the arms of a chair. The confederate then goes to the bowl of fruit, takes the apple with the piece missing and puts it in your right hand. He is careful to keep the side of the apple with the missing piece from audience view.

When the lights are turned out, toss the apple from the right hand and catch it in the left. Have the lights turned on again. Then show that although your hands were tied, you managed to take a bite from the apple even as it went from right to left in the darkness.

A CATALOG OF SELECTED

DOVER BOOKS

IN ALL FIELDS OF INTEREST

A CATALOG OF SELECTED DOVER
BOOKS IN ALL FIELDS OF INTEREST

CONCERNING THE SPIRITUAL IN ART, Wassily Kandinsky. Pioneering work by father of abstract art. Thoughts on color theory, nature of art. Analysis of earlier masters. 12 illustrations. 80pp. of text. 5⅜ x 8½. 23411-8 Pa. $3.95

ANIMALS: 1,419 Copyright-Free Illustrations of Mammals, Birds, Fish, Insects, etc., Jim Harter (ed.). Clear wood engravings present, in extremely lifelike poses, over 1,000 species of animals. One of the most extensive pictorial sourcebooks of its kind. Captions. Index. 284pp. 9 x 12. 23766-4 Pa. $12.95

CELTIC ART: The Methods of Construction, George Bain. Simple geometric techniques for making Celtic interlacements, spirals, Kells-type initials, animals, humans, etc. Over 500 illustrations. 160pp. 9 x 12. (USO) 22923-8 Pa. $9.95

AN ATLAS OF ANATOMY FOR ARTISTS, Fritz Schider. Most thorough reference work on art anatomy in the world. Hundreds of illustrations, including selections from works by Vesalius, Leonardo, Goya, Ingres, Michelangelo, others. 593 illustrations. 192pp. 7⅛ x 10¼. 20241-0 Pa. $9.95

CELTIC HAND STROKE-BY-STROKE (Irish Half-Uncial from "The Book of Kells"): An Arthur Baker Calligraphy Manual, Arthur Baker. Complete guide to creating each letter of the alphabet in distinctive Celtic manner. Covers hand position, strokes, pens, inks, paper, more. Illustrated. 48pp. 8¼ x 11. 24336-2 Pa. $3.95

EASY ORIGAMI, John Montroll. Charming collection of 32 projects (hat, cup, pelican, piano, swan, many more) specially designed for the novice origami hobbyist. Clearly illustrated easy-to-follow instructions insure that even beginning papercrafters will achieve successful results. 48pp. 8¼ x 11. 27298-2 Pa. $3.50

THE COMPLETE BOOK OF BIRDHOUSE CONSTRUCTION FOR WOODWORKERS, Scott D. Campbell. Detailed instructions, illustrations, tables. Also data on bird habitat and instinct patterns. Bibliography. 3 tables. 63 illustrations in 15 figures. 48pp. 5¼ x 8½. 24407-5 Pa. $2.50

BLOOMINGDALE'S ILLUSTRATED 1886 CATALOG: Fashions, Dry Goods and Housewares, Bloomingdale Brothers. Famed merchants' extremely rare catalog depicting about 1,700 products: clothing, housewares, firearms, dry goods, jewelry, more. Invaluable for dating, identifying vintage items. Also, copyright-free graphics for artists, designers. Co-published with Henry Ford Museum & Greenfield Village. 160pp. 8¼ x 11. 25780-0 Pa. $10.95

HISTORIC COSTUME IN PICTURES, Braun & Schneider. Over 1,450 costumed figures in clearly detailed engravings–from dawn of civilization to end of 19th century. Captions. Many folk costumes. 256pp. 8⅜ x 11¾. 23150-X Pa. $12.95

STICKLEY CRAFTSMAN FURNITURE CATALOGS, Gustav Stickley and L. & J. G. Stickley. Beautiful, functional furniture in two authentic catalogs from 1910. 594 illustrations, including 277 photos, show settles, rockers, armchairs, reclining chairs, bookcases, desks, tables. 183pp. 6½ x 9¼. 23838-5 Pa. $9.95

AMERICAN LOCOMOTIVES IN HISTORIC PHOTOGRAPHS: 1858 to 1949, Ron Ziel (ed.). A rare collection of 126 meticulously detailed official photographs, called "builder portraits," of American locomotives that majestically chronicle the rise of steam locomotive power in America. Introduction. Detailed captions. xi + 129pp. 9 x 12. 27393-8 Pa. $12.95

AMERICA'S LIGHTHOUSES: An Illustrated History, Francis Ross Holland, Jr. Delightfully written, profusely illustrated fact-filled survey of over 200 American lighthouses since 1716. History, anecdotes, technological advances, more. 240pp. 8 x 10¾. 25576-X Pa. $12.95

TOWARDS A NEW ARCHITECTURE, Le Corbusier. Pioneering manifesto by founder of "International School." Technical and aesthetic theories, views of industry, economics, relation of form to function, "mass-production split" and much more. Profusely illustrated. 320pp. 6⅛ x 9¼. (USO) 25023-7 Pa. $9.95

HOW THE OTHER HALF LIVES, Jacob Riis. Famous journalistic record, exposing poverty and degradation of New York slums around 1900, by major social reformer. 100 striking and influential photographs. 233pp. 10 x 7⅞. 22012-5 Pa. $10.95

FRUIT KEY AND TWIG KEY TO TREES AND SHRUBS, William M. Harlow. One of the handiest and most widely used identification aids. Fruit key covers 120 deciduous and evergreen species; twig key 160 deciduous species. Easily used. Over 300 photographs. 126pp. 5⅜ x 8½. 20511-8 Pa. $3.95

COMMON BIRD SONGS, Dr. Donald J. Borror. Songs of 60 most common U.S. birds: robins, sparrows, cardinals, bluejays, finches, more—arranged in order of increasing complexity. Up to 9 variations of songs of each species.
Cassette and manual 99911-4 $8.95

ORCHIDS AS HOUSE PLANTS, Rebecca Tyson Northen. Grow cattleyas and many other kinds of orchids—in a window, in a case, or under artificial light. 63 illustrations. 148pp. 5⅜ x 8½. 23261-1 Pa. $4.95

MONSTER MAZES, Dave Phillips. Masterful mazes at four levels of difficulty. Avoid deadly perils and evil creatures to find magical treasures. Solutions for all 32 exciting illustrated puzzles. 48pp. 8¼ x 11. 26005-4 Pa. $2.95

MOZART'S DON GIOVANNI (DOVER OPERA LIBRETTO SERIES), Wolfgang Amadeus Mozart. Introduced and translated by Ellen H. Bleiler. Standard Italian libretto, with complete English translation. Convenient and thoroughly portable—an ideal companion for reading along with a recording or the performance itself. Introduction. List of characters. Plot summary. 121pp. 5¼ x 8½. 24944-1 Pa. $2.95

TECHNICAL MANUAL AND DICTIONARY OF CLASSICAL BALLET, Gail Grant. Defines, explains, comments on steps, movements, poses and concepts. 15-page pictorial section. Basic book for student, viewer. 127pp. 5⅜ x 8½. 21843-0 Pa. $4.95

BRASS INSTRUMENTS: Their History and Development, Anthony Baines. Authoritative, updated survey of the evolution of trumpets, trombones, bugles, cornets, French horns, tubas and other brass wind instruments. Over 140 illustrations and 48 music examples. Corrected and updated by author. New preface. Bibliography. 320pp. 5⅜ x 8½. 27574-4 Pa. $9.95

HOLLYWOOD GLAMOR PORTRAITS, John Kobal (ed.). 145 photos from 1926-49. Harlow, Gable, Bogart, Bacall; 94 stars in all. Full background on photographers, technical aspects. 160pp. 8⅜ x 11¼. 23352-9 Pa. $12.95

MAX AND MORITZ, Wilhelm Busch. Great humor classic in both German and English. Also 10 other works: "Cat and Mouse," "Plisch and Plumm," etc. 216pp. 5⅜ x 8½. 20181-3 Pa. $6.95

THE RAVEN AND OTHER FAVORITE POEMS, Edgar Allan Poe. Over 40 of the author's most memorable poems: "The Bells," "Ulalume," "Israfel," "To Helen," "The Conqueror Worm," "Eldorado," "Annabel Lee," many more. Alphabetic lists of titles and first lines. 64pp. 5³⁄₁₆ x 8¼. 26685-0 Pa. $1.00

PERSONAL MEMOIRS OF U. S. GRANT, Ulysses Simpson Grant. Intelligent, deeply moving firsthand account of Civil War campaigns, considered by many the finest military memoirs ever written. Includes letters, historic photographs, maps and more. 528pp. 6⅛ x 9¼. 28587-1 Pa. $11.95

AMULETS AND SUPERSTITIONS, E. A. Wallis Budge. Comprehensive discourse on origin, powers of amulets in many ancient cultures: Arab, Persian Babylonian, Assyrian, Egyptian, Gnostic, Hebrew, Phoenician, Syriac, etc. Covers cross, swastika, crucifix, seals, rings, stones, etc. 584pp. 5⅜ x 8½. 23573-4 Pa. $12.95

RUSSIAN STORIES/PYCCKNE PACCKA3bl: A Dual-Language Book, edited by Gleb Struve. Twelve tales by such masters as Chekhov, Tolstoy, Dostoevsky, Pushkin, others. Excellent word-for-word English translations on facing pages, plus teaching and study aids, Russian/English vocabulary, biographical/critical introductions, more. 416pp. 5⅜ x 8½. 26244-8 Pa. $8.95

PHILADELPHIA THEN AND NOW: 60 Sites Photographed in the Past and Present, Kenneth Finkel and Susan Oyama. Rare photographs of City Hall, Logan Square, Independence Hall, Betsy Ross House, other landmarks juxtaposed with contemporary views. Captures changing face of historic city. Introduction. Captions. 128pp. 8¼ x 11. 25790-8 Pa. $9.95

AIA ARCHITECTURAL GUIDE TO NASSAU AND SUFFOLK COUNTIES, LONG ISLAND, The American Institute of Architects, Long Island Chapter, and the Society for the Preservation of Long Island Antiquities. Comprehensive, well-researched and generously illustrated volume brings to life over three centuries of Long Island's great architectural heritage. More than 240 photographs with authoritative, extensively detailed captions. 176pp. 8¼ x 11. 26946-9 Pa. $14.95

NORTH AMERICAN INDIAN LIFE: Customs and Traditions of 23 Tribes, Elsie Clews Parsons (ed.). 27 fictionalized essays by noted anthropologists examine religion, customs, government, additional facets of life among the Winnebago, Crow, Zuni, Eskimo, other tribes. 480pp. 6⅛ x 9¼. 27377-6 Pa. $10.95

FRANK LLOYD WRIGHT'S HOLLYHOCK HOUSE, Donald Hoffmann. Lavishly illustrated, carefully documented study of one of Wright's most controversial residential designs. Over 120 photographs, floor plans, elevations, etc. Detailed perceptive text by noted Wright scholar. Index. 128pp. 9¼ x 10¾. 27133-1 Pa. $11.95

THE MALE AND FEMALE FIGURE IN MOTION: 60 Classic Photographic Sequences, Eadweard Muybridge. 60 true-action photographs of men and women walking, running, climbing, bending, turning, etc., reproduced from rare 19th-century masterpiece. vi + 121pp. 9 x 12. 24745-7 Pa. $10.95

1001 QUESTIONS ANSWERED ABOUT THE SEASHORE, N. J. Berrill and Jacquelyn Berrill. Queries answered about dolphins, sea snails, sponges, starfish, fishes, shore birds, many others. Covers appearance, breeding, growth, feeding, much more. 305pp. 5¼ x 8¼. 23366-9 Pa. $8.95

GUIDE TO OWL WATCHING IN NORTH AMERICA, Donald S. Heintzelman. Superb guide offers complete data and descriptions of 19 species: barn owl, screech owl, snowy owl, many more. Expert coverage of owl-watching equipment, conservation, migrations and invasions, etc. Guide to observing sites. 84 illustrations. xiii + 193pp. 5⅜ x 8½. 27344-X Pa. $8.95

MEDICINAL AND OTHER USES OF NORTH AMERICAN PLANTS: A Historical Survey with Special Reference to the Eastern Indian Tribes, Charlotte Erichsen-Brown. Chronological historical citations document 500 years of usage of plants, trees, shrubs native to eastern Canada, northeastern U.S. Also complete identifying information. 343 illustrations. 544pp. 6½ x 9¼. 25951-X Pa. $12.95

STORYBOOK MAZES, Dave Phillips. 23 stories and mazes on two-page spreads: Wizard of Oz, Treasure Island, Robin Hood, etc. Solutions. 64pp. 8¼ x 11. 23628-5 Pa. $2.95

NEGRO FOLK MUSIC, U.S.A., Harold Courlander. Noted folklorist's scholarly yet readable analysis of rich and varied musical tradition. Includes authentic versions of over 40 folk songs. Valuable bibliography and discography. xi + 324pp. 5⅜ x 8½. 27350-4 Pa. $9.95

MOVIE-STAR PORTRAITS OF THE FORTIES, John Kobal (ed.). 163 glamor, studio photos of 106 stars of the 1940s: Rita Hayworth, Ava Gardner, Marlon Brando, Clark Gable, many more. 176pp. 8⅜ x 11¼. 23546-7 Pa. $12.95

BENCHLEY LOST AND FOUND, Robert Benchley. Finest humor from early 30s, about pet peeves, child psychologists, post office and others. Mostly unavailable elsewhere. 73 illustrations by Peter Arno and others. 183pp. 5⅜ x 8½. 22410-4 Pa. $6.95

YEKL and THE IMPORTED BRIDEGROOM AND OTHER STORIES OF YIDDISH NEW YORK, Abraham Cahan. Film Hester Street based on Yekl (1896). Novel, other stories among first about Jewish immigrants on N.Y.'s East Side. 240pp. 5⅜ x 8½. 22427-9 Pa. $6.95

SELECTED POEMS, Walt Whitman. Generous sampling from *Leaves of Grass*. Twenty-four poems include "I Hear America Singing," "Song of the Open Road," "I Sing the Body Electric," "When Lilacs Last in the Dooryard Bloom'd," "O Captain! My Captain!"–all reprinted from an authoritative edition. Lists of titles and first lines. 128pp. 5³⁄₁₆ x 8¼. 26878-0 Pa. $1.00

THE BEST TALES OF HOFFMANN, E. T. A. Hoffmann. 10 of Hoffmann's most important stories: "Nutcracker and the King of Mice," "The Golden Flowerpot," etc. 458pp. 5⅜ x 8½. 21793-0 Pa. $9.95

FROM FETISH TO GOD IN ANCIENT EGYPT, E. A. Wallis Budge. Rich detailed survey of Egyptian conception of "God" and gods, magic, cult of animals, Osiris, more. Also, superb English translations of hymns and legends. 240 illustrations. 545pp. 5⅜ x 8½. 25803-3 Pa. $13.95

FRENCH STORIES/CONTES FRANÇAIS: A Dual-Language Book, Wallace Fowlie. Ten stories by French masters, Voltaire to Camus: "Micromegas" by Voltaire; "The Atheist's Mass" by Balzac; "Minuet" by de Maupassant; "The Guest" by Camus, six more. Excellent English translations on facing pages. Also French-English vocabulary list, exercises, more. 352pp. 5⅜ x 8½. 26443-2 Pa. $8.95

CHICAGO AT THE TURN OF THE CENTURY IN PHOTOGRAPHS: 122 Historic Views from the Collections of the Chicago Historical Society, Larry A. Viskochil. Rare large-format prints offer detailed views of City Hall, State Street, the Loop, Hull House, Union Station, many other landmarks, circa 1904-1913. Introduction. Captions. Maps. 144pp. 9⅜ x 12¼. 24656-6 Pa. $12.95

OLD BROOKLYN IN EARLY PHOTOGRAPHS, 1865-1929, William Lee Younger. Luna Park, Gravesend race track, construction of Grand Army Plaza, moving of Hotel Brighton, etc. 157 previously unpublished photographs. 165pp. 8⅞ x 11¾. 23587-4 Pa. $13.95

THE MYTHS OF THE NORTH AMERICAN INDIANS, Lewis Spence. Rich anthology of the myths and legends of the Algonquins, Iroquois, Pawnees and Sioux, prefaced by an extensive historical and ethnological commentary. 36 illustrations. 480pp. 5⅜ x 8½. 25967-6 Pa. $8.95

AN ENCYCLOPEDIA OF BATTLES: Accounts of Over 1,560 Battles from 1479 B.C. to the Present, David Eggenberger. Essential details of every major battle in recorded history from the first battle of Megiddo in 1479 B.C. to Grenada in 1984. List of Battle Maps. New Appendix covering the years 1967-1984. Index. 99 illustrations. 544pp. 6½ x 9¼. 24913-1 Pa. $14.95

SAILING ALONE AROUND THE WORLD, Captain Joshua Slocum. First man to sail around the world, alone, in small boat. One of great feats of seamanship told in delightful manner. 67 illustrations. 294pp. 5⅜ x 8½. 20326-3 Pa. $5.95

ANARCHISM AND OTHER ESSAYS, Emma Goldman. Powerful, penetrating, prophetic essays on direct action, role of minorities, prison reform, puritan hypocrisy, violence, etc. 271pp. 5⅜ x 8½. 22484-8 Pa. $6.95

MYTHS OF THE HINDUS AND BUDDHISTS, Ananda K. Coomaraswamy and Sister Nivedita. Great stories of the epics; deeds of Krishna, Shiva, taken from puranas, Vedas, folk tales; etc. 32 illustrations. 400pp. 5⅜ x 8½. 21759-0 Pa. $10.95

BEYOND PSYCHOLOGY, Otto Rank. Fear of death, desire of immortality, nature of sexuality, social organization, creativity, according to Rankian system. 291pp. 5⅜ x 8½. 20485-5 Pa. $8.95

A THEOLOGICO-POLITICAL TREATISE, Benedict Spinoza. Also contains unfinished Political Treatise. Great classic on religious liberty, theory of government on common consent. R. Elwes translation. Total of 421pp. 5⅜ x 8½. 20249-6 Pa. $9.95

CATALOG OF DOVER BOOKS

MY BONDAGE AND MY FREEDOM, Frederick Douglass. Born a slave, Douglass became outspoken force in antislavery movement. The best of Douglass' autobiographies. Graphic description of slave life. 464pp. 5⅜ x 8½. 22457-0 Pa. $8.95

FOLLOWING THE EQUATOR: A Journey Around the World, Mark Twain. Fascinating humorous account of 1897 voyage to Hawaii, Australia, India, New Zealand, etc. Ironic, bemused reports on peoples, customs, climate, flora and fauna, politics, much more. 197 illustrations. 720pp. 5⅜ x 8½. 26113-1 Pa. $15.95

THE PEOPLE CALLED SHAKERS, Edward D. Andrews. Definitive study of Shakers: origins, beliefs, practices, dances, social organization, furniture and crafts, etc. 33 illustrations. 351pp. 5⅜ x 8½. 21081-2 Pa. $8.95

THE MYTHS OF GREECE AND ROME, H. A. Guerber. A classic of mythology, generously illustrated, long prized for its simple, graphic, accurate retelling of the principal myths of Greece and Rome, and for its commentary on their origins and significance. With 64 illustrations by Michelangelo, Raphael, Titian, Rubens, Canova, Bernini and others. 480pp. 5⅜ x 8½. 27584-1 Pa. $9.95

PSYCHOLOGY OF MUSIC, Carl E. Seashore. Classic work discusses music as a medium from psychological viewpoint. Clear treatment of physical acoustics, auditory apparatus, sound perception, development of musical skills, nature of musical feeling, host of other topics. 88 figures. 408pp. 5⅜ x 8½. 21851-1 Pa. $10.95

THE PHILOSOPHY OF HISTORY, Georg W. Hegel. Great classic of Western thought develops concept that history is not chance but rational process, the evolution of freedom. 457pp. 5⅜ x 8½. 20112-0 Pa. $9.95

THE BOOK OF TEA, Kakuzo Okakura. Minor classic of the Orient: entertaining, charming explanation, interpretation of traditional Japanese culture in terms of tea ceremony. 94pp. 5⅜ x 8½. 20070-1 Pa. $3.95

LIFE IN ANCIENT EGYPT, Adolf Erman. Fullest, most thorough, detailed older account with much not in more recent books, domestic life, religion, magic, medicine, commerce, much more. Many illustrations reproduce tomb paintings, carvings, hieroglyphs, etc. 597pp. 5⅜ x 8½. 22632-8 Pa. $11.95

SUNDIALS, Their Theory and Construction, Albert Waugh. Far and away the best, most thorough coverage of ideas, mathematics concerned, types, construction, adjusting anywhere. Simple, nontechnical treatment allows even children to build several of these dials. Over 100 illustrations. 230pp. 5⅜ x 8½. 22947-5 Pa. $7.95

DYNAMICS OF FLUIDS IN POROUS MEDIA, Jacob Bear. For advanced students of ground water hydrology, soil mechanics and physics, drainage and irrigation engineering, and more. 335 illustrations. Exercises, with answers. 784pp. 6⅛ x 9¼. 65675-6 Pa. $19.95

SONGS OF EXPERIENCE: Facsimile Reproduction with 26 Plates in Full Color, William Blake. 26 full-color plates from a rare 1826 edition. Includes "TheTyger," "London," "Holy Thursday," and other poems. Printed text of poems. 48pp. 5¼ x 7. 24636-1 Pa. $4.95

OLD-TIME VIGNETTES IN FULL COLOR, Carol Belanger Grafton (ed.). Over 390 charming, often sentimental illustrations, selected from archives of Victorian graphics–pretty women posing, children playing, food, flowers, kittens and puppies, smiling cherubs, birds and butterflies, much more. All copyright-free. 48pp. 9¼ x 12¼. 27269-9 Pa. $7.95

PERSPECTIVE FOR ARTISTS, Rex Vicat Cole. Depth, perspective of sky and sea, shadows, much more, not usually covered. 391 diagrams, 81 reproductions of drawings and paintings. 279pp. 5⅜ x 8½. 22487-2 Pa. $7.95

DRAWING THE LIVING FIGURE, Joseph Sheppard. Innovative approach to artistic anatomy focuses on specifics of surface anatomy, rather than muscles and bones. Over 170 drawings of live models in front, back and side views, and in widely varying poses. Accompanying diagrams. 177 illustrations. Introduction. Index. 144pp. 8⅜ x11¼. 26723-7 Pa. $8.95

GOTHIC AND OLD ENGLISH ALPHABETS: 100 Complete Fonts, Dan X. Solo. Add power, elegance to posters, signs, other graphics with 100 stunning copyright-free alphabets: Blackstone, Dolbey, Germania, 97 more–including many lower-case, numerals, punctuation marks. 104pp. 8⅛ x 11. 24695-7 Pa. $8.95

HOW TO DO BEADWORK, Mary White. Fundamental book on craft from simple projects to five-bead chains and woven works. 106 illustrations. 142pp. 5⅜ x 8. 20697-1 Pa. $4.95

THE BOOK OF WOOD CARVING, Charles Marshall Sayers. Finest book for beginners discusses fundamentals and offers 34 designs. "Absolutely first rate . . . well thought out and well executed."–E. J. Tangerman. 118pp. 7¾ x 10⅝. 23654-4 Pa. $6.95

ILLUSTRATED CATALOG OF CIVIL WAR MILITARY GOODS: Union Army Weapons, Insignia, Uniform Accessories, and Other Equipment, Schuyler, Hartley, and Graham. Rare, profusely illustrated 1846 catalog includes Union Army uniform and dress regulations, arms and ammunition, coats, insignia, flags, swords, rifles, etc. 226 illustrations. 160pp. 9 x 12. 24939-5 Pa. $10.95

WOMEN'S FASHIONS OF THE EARLY 1900s: An Unabridged Republication of "New York Fashions, 1909," National Cloak & Suit Co. Rare catalog of mail-order fashions documents women's and children's clothing styles shortly after the turn of the century. Captions offer full descriptions, prices. Invaluable resource for fashion, costume historians. Approximately 725 illustrations. 128pp. 8⅜ x 11¼. 27276-1 Pa. $11.95

THE 1912 AND 1915 GUSTAV STICKLEY FURNITURE CATALOGS, Gustav Stickley. With over 200 detailed illustrations and descriptions, these two catalogs are essential reading and reference materials and identification guides for Stickley furniture. Captions cite materials, dimensions and prices. 112pp. 6½ x 9¼. 26676-1 Pa. $9.95

EARLY AMERICAN LOCOMOTIVES, John H. White, Jr. Finest locomotive engravings from early 19th century: historical (1804–74), main-line (after 1870), special, foreign, etc. 147 plates. 142pp. 11⅜ x 8¼. 22772-3 Pa. $10.95

THE TALL SHIPS OF TODAY IN PHOTOGRAPHS, Frank O. Braynard. Lavishly illustrated tribute to nearly 100 majestic contemporary sailing vessels: Amerigo Vespucci, Clearwater, Constitution, Eagle, Mayflower, Sea Cloud, Victory, many more. Authoritative captions provide statistics, background on each ship. 190 black-and-white photographs and illustrations. Introduction. 128pp. 8⅞ x 11¾. 27163-3 Pa. $13.95

EARLY NINETEENTH-CENTURY CRAFTS AND TRADES, Peter Stockham (ed.). Extremely rare 1807 volume describes to youngsters the crafts and trades of the day: brickmaker, weaver, dressmaker, bookbinder, ropemaker, saddler, many more. Quaint prose, charming illustrations for each craft. 20 black-and-white line illustrations. 192pp. 4⅝ x 6. 27293-1 Pa. $4.95

VICTORIAN FASHIONS AND COSTUMES FROM HARPER'S BAZAR, 1867–1898, Stella Blum (ed.). Day costumes, evening wear, sports clothes, shoes, hats, other accessories in over 1,000 detailed engravings. 320pp. 9⅜ x 12¼. 22990-4 Pa. $14.95

GUSTAV STICKLEY, THE CRAFTSMAN, Mary Ann Smith. Superb study surveys broad scope of Stickley's achievement, especially in architecture. Design philosophy, rise and fall of the Craftsman empire, descriptions and floor plans for many Craftsman houses, more. 86 black-and-white halftones. 31 line illustrations. Introduction 208pp. 6½ x 9¼. 27210-9 Pa. $9.95

THE LONG ISLAND RAIL ROAD IN EARLY PHOTOGRAPHS, Ron Ziel. Over 220 rare photos, informative text document origin (1844) and development of rail service on Long Island. Vintage views of early trains, locomotives, stations, passengers, crews, much more. Captions. 8⅞ x 11¾. 26301-0 Pa. $13.95

THE BOOK OF OLD SHIPS: From Egyptian Galleys to Clipper Ships, Henry B. Culver. Superb, authoritative history of sailing vessels, with 80 magnificent line illustrations. Galley, bark, caravel, longship, whaler, many more. Detailed, informative text on each vessel by noted naval historian. Introduction. 256pp. 5⅜ x 8½. 27332-6 Pa. $7.95

TEN BOOKS ON ARCHITECTURE, Vitruvius. The most important book ever written on architecture. Early Roman aesthetics, technology, classical orders, site selection, all other aspects. Morgan translation. 331pp. 5⅜ x 8½. 20645-9 Pa. $8.95

THE HUMAN FIGURE IN MOTION, Eadweard Muybridge. More than 4,500 stopped-action photos, in action series, showing undraped men, women, children jumping, lying down, throwing, sitting, wrestling, carrying, etc. 390pp. 7⅞ x 10⅝. 20204-6 Clothbd. $25.95

TREES OF THE EASTERN AND CENTRAL UNITED STATES AND CANADA, William M. Harlow. Best one-volume guide to 140 trees. Full descriptions, woodlore, range, etc. Over 600 illustrations. Handy size. 288pp. 4½ x 6⅜. 20395-6 Pa. $6.95

SONGS OF WESTERN BIRDS, Dr. Donald J. Borror. Complete song and call repertoire of 60 western species, including flycatchers, juncoes, cactus wrens, many more–includes fully illustrated booklet. Cassette and manual 99913-0 $8.95

GROWING AND USING HERBS AND SPICES, Milo Miloradovich. Versatile handbook provides all the information needed for cultivation and use of all the herbs and spices available in North America. 4 illustrations. Index. Glossary. 236pp. 5⅜ x 8½. 25058-X Pa. $6.95

BIG BOOK OF MAZES AND LABYRINTHS, Walter Shepherd. 50 mazes and labyrinths in all–classical, solid, ripple, and more–in one great volume. Perfect inexpensive puzzler for clever youngsters. Full solutions. 112pp. 8⅛ x 11. 22951-3 Pa. $4.95

CATALOG OF DOVER BOOKS

PIANO TUNING, J. Cree Fischer. Clearest, best book for beginner, amateur. Simple repairs, raising dropped notes, tuning by easy method of flattened fifths. No previous skills needed. 4 illustrations. 201pp. 5⅜ x 8½. 23267-0 Pa. $6.95

A SOURCE BOOK IN THEATRICAL HISTORY, A. M. Nagler. Contemporary observers on acting, directing, make-up, costuming, stage props, machinery, scene design, from Ancient Greece to Chekhov. 611pp. 5⅜ x 8½. 20515-0 Pa. $12.95

THE COMPLETE NONSENSE OF EDWARD LEAR, Edward Lear. All nonsense limericks, zany alphabets, Owl and Pussycat, songs, nonsense botany, etc., illustrated by Lear. Total of 320pp. 5⅜ x 8½. (USO) 20167-8 Pa. $6.95

VICTORIAN PARLOUR POETRY: An Annotated Anthology, Michael R. Turner. 117 gems by Longfellow, Tennyson, Browning, many lesser-known poets. "The Village Blacksmith," "Curfew Must Not Ring Tonight," "Only a Baby Small," dozens more, often difficult to find elsewhere. Index of poets, titles, first lines. xxiii + 325pp. 5⅜ x 8¼. 27044-0 Pa. $8.95

DUBLINERS, James Joyce. Fifteen stories offer vivid, tightly focused observations of the lives of Dublin's poorer classes. At least one, "The Dead," is considered a masterpiece. Reprinted complete and unabridged from standard edition. 160pp. 5³⁄₁₆ x 8¼. 26870-5 Pa. $1.00

THE HAUNTED MONASTERY and THE CHINESE MAZE MURDERS, Robert van Gulik. Two full novels by van Gulik, set in 7th-century China, continue adventures of Judge Dee and his companions. An evil Taoist monastery, seemingly supernatural events; overgrown topiary maze hides strange crimes. 27 illustrations. 328pp. 5⅜ x 8½. 23502-5 Pa. $8.95

THE BOOK OF THE SACRED MAGIC OF ABRAMELIN THE MAGE, translated by S. MacGregor Mathers. Medieval manuscript of ceremonial magic. Basic document in Aleister Crowley, Golden Dawn groups. 268pp. 5⅜ x 8½. 23211-5 Pa. $8.95

NEW RUSSIAN-ENGLISH AND ENGLISH-RUSSIAN DICTIONARY, M. A. O'Brien. This is a remarkably handy Russian dictionary, containing a surprising amount of information, including over 70,000 entries. 366pp. 4½ x 6⅛. 20208-9 Pa. $9.95

HISTORIC HOMES OF THE AMERICAN PRESIDENTS, Second, Revised Edition, Irvin Haas. A traveler's guide to American Presidential homes, most open to the public, depicting and describing homes occupied by every American President from George Washington to George Bush. With visiting hours, admission charges, travel routes. 175 photographs. Index. 160pp. 8¼ x 11. 26751-2 Pa. $11.95

NEW YORK IN THE FORTIES, Andreas Feininger. 162 brilliant photographs by the well-known photographer, formerly with *Life* magazine. Commuters, shoppers, Times Square at night, much else from city at its peak. Captions by John von Hartz. 181pp. 9¼ x 10¾. 23585-8 Pa. $12.95

INDIAN SIGN LANGUAGE, William Tomkins. Over 525 signs developed by Sioux and other tribes. Written instructions and diagrams. Also 290 pictographs. 111pp. 6⅛ x 9¼. 22029-X Pa. $3.95

ANATOMY: A Complete Guide for Artists, Joseph Sheppard. A master of figure drawing shows artists how to render human anatomy convincingly. Over 460 illustrations. 224pp. 8⅜ x 11¼. 27279-6 Pa. $10.95

MEDIEVAL CALLIGRAPHY: Its History and Technique, Marc Drogin. Spirited history, comprehensive instruction manual covers 13 styles (ca. 4th century thru 15th). Excellent photographs; directions for duplicating medieval techniques with modern tools. 224pp. 8⅜ x 11¼. 26142-5 Pa. $12.95

DRIED FLOWERS: How to Prepare Them, Sarah Whitlock and Martha Rankin. Complete instructions on how to use silica gel, meal and borax, perlite aggregate, sand and borax, glycerine and water to create attractive permanent flower arrangements. 12 illustrations. 32pp. 5⅜ x 8½. 21802-3 Pa. $1.00

EASY-TO-MAKE BIRD FEEDERS FOR WOODWORKERS, Scott D. Campbell. Detailed, simple-to-use guide for designing, constructing, caring for and using feeders. Text, illustrations for 12 classic and contemporary designs. 96pp. 5⅜ x 8½. 25847-5 Pa. $2.95

SCOTTISH WONDER TALES FROM MYTH AND LEGEND, Donald A. Mackenzie. 16 lively tales tell of giants rumbling down mountainsides, of a magic wand that turns stone pillars into warriors, of gods and goddesses, evil hags, powerful forces and more. 240pp. 5⅜ x 8½. 29677-6 Pa. $6.95

THE HISTORY OF UNDERCLOTHES, C. Willett Cunnington and Phyllis Cunnington. Fascinating, well-documented survey covering six centuries of English undergarments, enhanced with over 100 illustrations: 12th-century laced-up bodice, footed long drawers (1795), 19th-century bustles, 19th-century corsets for men, Victorian "bust improvers," much more. 272pp. 5⅝ x 8¼. 27124-2 Pa. $9.95

ARTS AND CRAFTS FURNITURE: The Complete Brooks Catalog of 1912, Brooks Manufacturing Co. Photos and detailed descriptions of more than 150 now very collectible furniture designs from the Arts and Crafts movement depict davenports, settees, buffets, desks, tables, chairs, bedsteads, dressers and more, all built of solid, quarter-sawed oak. Invaluable for students and enthusiasts of antiques, Americana and the decorative arts. 80pp. 6½ x 9¼. 27471-3 Pa. $8.95

HOW WE INVENTED THE AIRPLANE: An Illustrated History, Orville Wright. Fascinating firsthand account covers early experiments, construction of planes and motors, first flights, much more. Introduction and commentary by Fred C. Kelly. 76 photographs. 96pp. 8¼ x 11. 25662-6 Pa. $8.95

THE ARTS OF THE SAILOR: Knotting, Splicing and Ropework, Hervey Garrett Smith. Indispensable shipboard reference covers tools, basic knots and useful hitches; handsewing and canvas work, more. Over 100 illustrations. Delightful reading for sea lovers. 256pp. 5⅜ x 8½. 26440-8 Pa. $7.95

FRANK LLOYD WRIGHT'S FALLINGWATER: The House and Its History, Second, Revised Edition, Donald Hoffmann. A total revision–both in text and illustrations–of the standard document on Fallingwater, the boldest, most personal architectural statement of Wright's mature years, updated with valuable new material from the recently opened Frank Lloyd Wright Archives. "Fascinating"–*The New York Times*. 116 illustrations. 128pp. 9¼ x 10¾. 27430-6 Pa. $11.95

PHOTOGRAPHIC SKETCHBOOK OF THE CIVIL WAR, Alexander Gardner. 100 photos taken on field during the Civil War. Famous shots of Manassas Harper's Ferry, Lincoln, Richmond, slave pens, etc. 244pp. 10⅝ x 8¼. 22731-6 Pa. $9.95

FIVE ACRES AND INDEPENDENCE, Maurice G. Kains. Great back-to-the-land classic explains basics of self-sufficient farming. The one book to get. 95 illustrations. 397pp. 5⅜ x 8½. 20974-1 Pa. $7.95

SONGS OF EASTERN BIRDS, Dr. Donald J. Borror. Songs and calls of 60 species most common to eastern U.S.: warblers, woodpeckers, flycatchers, thrushes, larks, many more in high-quality recording. Cassette and manual 99912-2 $9.95

A MODERN HERBAL, Margaret Grieve. Much the fullest, most exact, most useful compilation of herbal material. Gigantic alphabetical encyclopedia, from aconite to zedoary, gives botanical information, medical properties, folklore, economic uses, much else. Indispensable to serious reader. 161 illustrations. 888pp. 6½ x 9¼. 2-vol. set. (USO) Vol. I: 22798-7 Pa. $9.95
Vol. II: 22799-5 Pa. $9.95

HIDDEN TREASURE MAZE BOOK, Dave Phillips. Solve 34 challenging mazes accompanied by heroic tales of adventure. Evil dragons, people-eating plants, bloodthirsty giants, many more dangerous adversaries lurk at every twist and turn. 34 mazes, stories, solutions. 48pp. 8¼ x 11. 24566-7 Pa. $2.95

LETTERS OF W. A. MOZART, Wolfgang A. Mozart. Remarkable letters show bawdy wit, humor, imagination, musical insights, contemporary musical world; includes some letters from Leopold Mozart. 276pp. 5⅜ x 8½. 22859-2 Pa. $7.95

BASIC PRINCIPLES OF CLASSICAL BALLET, Agrippina Vaganova. Great Russian theoretician, teacher explains methods for teaching classical ballet. 118 illustrations. 175pp. 5⅜ x 8½. 22036-2 Pa. $5.95

THE JUMPING FROG, Mark Twain. Revenge edition. The original story of The Celebrated Jumping Frog of Calaveras County, a hapless French translation, and Twain's hilarious "retranslation" from the French. 12 illustrations. 66pp. 5⅜ x 8½. 22686-7 Pa. $3.95

BEST REMEMBERED POEMS, Martin Gardner (ed.). The 126 poems in this superb collection of 19th- and 20th-century British and American verse range from Shelley's "To a Skylark" to the impassioned "Renascence" of Edna St. Vincent Millay and to Edward Lear's whimsical "The Owl and the Pussycat." 224pp. 5⅜ x 8½. 27165-X Pa. $4.95

COMPLETE SONNETS, William Shakespeare. Over 150 exquisite poems deal with love, friendship, the tyranny of time, beauty's evanescence, death and other themes in language of remarkable power, precision and beauty. Glossary of archaic terms. 80pp. 5³⁄₁₆ x 8¼. 26686-9 Pa. $1.00

BODIES IN A BOOKSHOP, R. T. Campbell. Challenging mystery of blackmail and murder with ingenious plot and superbly drawn characters. In the best tradition of British suspense fiction. 192pp. 5⅜ x 8½. 24720-1 Pa. $6.95

THE WIT AND HUMOR OF OSCAR WILDE, Alvin Redman (ed.). More than 1,000 ripostes, paradoxes, wisecracks: Work is the curse of the drinking classes; I can resist everything except temptation; etc. 258pp. 5⅜ x 8½.　20602-5 Pa. $5.95

SHAKESPEARE LEXICON AND QUOTATION DICTIONARY, Alexander Schmidt. Full definitions, locations, shades of meaning in every word in plays and poems. More than 50,000 exact quotations. 1,485pp. 6½ x 9¼. 2-vol. set.
Vol. 1: 22726-X Pa. $16.95
Vol. 2: 22727-8 Pa. $16.95

SELECTED POEMS, Emily Dickinson. Over 100 best-known, best-loved poems by one of America's foremost poets, reprinted from authoritative early editions. No comparable edition at this price. Index of first lines. 64pp. 5³⁄₁₆ x 8¼.
26466-1 Pa. $1.00

CELEBRATED CASES OF JUDGE DEE (DEE GOONG AN), translated by Robert van Gulik. Authentic 18th-century Chinese detective novel; Dee and associates solve three interlocked cases. Led to van Gulik's own stories with same characters. Extensive introduction. 9 illustrations. 237pp. 5⅜ x 8½.　23337-5 Pa. $6.95

THE MALLEUS MALEFICARUM OF KRAMER AND SPRENGER, translated by Montague Summers. Full text of most important witchhunter's "bible," used by both Catholics and Protestants. 278pp. 6⅝ x 10.　22802-9 Pa. $12.95

SPANISH STORIES/CUENTOS ESPAÑOLES: A Dual-Language Book, Angel Flores (ed.). Unique format offers 13 great stories in Spanish by Cervantes, Borges, others. Faithful English translations on facing pages. 352pp. 5⅜ x 8½.
25399-6 Pa. $8.95

THE CHICAGO WORLD'S FAIR OF 1893: A Photographic Record, Stanley Appelbaum (ed.). 128 rare photos show 200 buildings, Beaux-Arts architecture, Midway, original Ferris Wheel, Edison's kinetoscope, more. Architectural emphasis; full text. 116pp. 8¼ x 11.　23990-X Pa. $9.95

OLD QUEENS, N.Y., IN EARLY PHOTOGRAPHS, Vincent F. Seyfried and William Asadorian. Over 160 rare photographs of Maspeth, Jamaica, Jackson Heights, and other areas. Vintage views of DeWitt Clinton mansion, 1939 World's Fair and more. Captions. 192pp. 8⅞ x 11.　26358-4 Pa. $12.95

CAPTURED BY THE INDIANS: 15 Firsthand Accounts, 1750-1870, Frederick Drimmer. Astounding true historical accounts of grisly torture, bloody conflicts, relentless pursuits, miraculous escapes and more, by people who lived to tell the tale. 384pp. 5⅜ x 8½.　24901-8 Pa. $8.95

THE WORLD'S GREAT SPEECHES, Lewis Copeland and Lawrence W. Lamm (eds.). Vast collection of 278 speeches of Greeks to 1970. Powerful and effective models; unique look at history. 842pp. 5⅜ x 8½.　20468-5 Pa. $14.95

THE BOOK OF THE SWORD, Sir Richard F. Burton. Great Victorian scholar/adventurer's eloquent, erudite history of the "queen of weapons"—from prehistory to early Roman Empire. Evolution and development of early swords, variations (sabre, broadsword, cutlass, scimitar, etc.), much more. 336pp. 6⅛ x 9¼.
25434-8 Pa. $9.95

AUTOBIOGRAPHY: The Story of My Experiments with Truth, Mohandas K. Gandhi. Boyhood, legal studies, purification, the growth of the Satyagraha (nonviolent protest) movement. Critical, inspiring work of the man responsible for the freedom of India. 480pp. 5⅜ x 8½. (USO)   24593-4 Pa. $8.95

CELTIC MYTHS AND LEGENDS, T. W. Rolleston. Masterful retelling of Irish and Welsh stories and tales. Cuchulain, King Arthur, Deirdre, the Grail, many more. First paperback edition. 58 full-page illustrations. 512pp. 5⅜ x 8½.   26507-2 Pa. $9.95

THE PRINCIPLES OF PSYCHOLOGY, William James. Famous long course complete, unabridged. Stream of thought, time perception, memory, experimental methods; great work decades ahead of its time. 94 figures. 1,391pp. 5⅜ x 8½. 2-vol. set.
Vol. I: 20381-6 Pa. $12.95
Vol. II: 20382-4 Pa. $12.95

THE WORLD AS WILL AND REPRESENTATION, Arthur Schopenhauer. Definitive English translation of Schopenhauer's life work, correcting more than 1,000 errors, omissions in earlier translations. Translated by E. F. J. Payne. Total of 1,269pp. 5⅜ x 8½. 2-vol. set.
Vol. 1: 21761-2 Pa. $11.95
Vol. 2: 21762-0 Pa. $12.95

MAGIC AND MYSTERY IN TIBET, Madame Alexandra David-Neel. Experiences among lamas, magicians, sages, sorcerers, Bonpa wizards. A true psychic discovery. 32 illustrations. 321pp. 5⅜ x 8½. (USO)   22682-4 Pa. $8.95

THE EGYPTIAN BOOK OF THE DEAD, E. A. Wallis Budge. Complete reproduction of Ani's papyrus, finest ever found. Full hieroglyphic text, interlinear transliteration, word-for-word translation, smooth translation. 533pp. 6½ x 9¼.
21866-X Pa. $10.95

MATHEMATICS FOR THE NONMATHEMATICIAN, Morris Kline. Detailed, college-level treatment of mathematics in cultural and historical context, with numerous exercises. Recommended Reading Lists. Tables. Numerous figures. 641pp. 5⅜ x 8½.
24823-2 Pa. $11.95

THEORY OF WING SECTIONS: Including a Summary of Airfoil Data, Ira H. Abbott and A. E. von Doenhoff. Concise compilation of subsonic aerodynamic characteristics of NACA wing sections, plus description of theory. 350pp. of tables. 693pp. 5⅜ x 8½.   60586-8 Pa. $14.95

THE RIME OF THE ANCIENT MARINER, Gustave Doré, S. T. Coleridge. Doré's finest work; 34 plates capture moods, subtleties of poem. Flawless full-size reproductions printed on facing pages with authoritative text of poem. "Beautiful. Simply beautiful."—*Publisher's Weekly.* 77pp. 9¼ x 12.   22305-1 Pa. $6.95

NORTH AMERICAN INDIAN DESIGNS FOR ARTISTS AND CRAFTSPEOPLE, Eva Wilson. Over 360 authentic copyright-free designs adapted from Navajo blankets, Hopi pottery, Sioux buffalo hides, more. Geometrics, symbolic figures, plant and animal motifs, etc. 128pp. 8⅜ x 11. (EUK)   25341-4 Pa. $8.95

SCULPTURE: Principles and Practice, Louis Slobodkin. Step-by-step approach to clay, plaster, metals, stone; classical and modern. 253 drawings, photos. 255pp. 8⅛ x 11.
22960-2 Pa. $11.95

THE INFLUENCE OF SEA POWER UPON HISTORY, 1660–1783, A. T. Mahan. Influential classic of naval history and tactics still used as text in war colleges. First paperback edition. 4 maps. 24 battle plans. 640pp. 5⅜ x 8½. 25509-3 Pa. $12.95

THE STORY OF THE TITANIC AS TOLD BY ITS SURVIVORS, Jack Winocour (ed.). What it was really like. Panic, despair, shocking inefficiency, and a little heroism. More thrilling than any fictional account. 26 illustrations. 320pp. 5⅜ x 8½. 20610-6 Pa. $8.95

FAIRY AND FOLK TALES OF THE IRISH PEASANTRY, William Butler Yeats (ed.). Treasury of 64 tales from the twilight world of Celtic myth and legend: "The Soul Cages," "The Kildare Pooka," "King O'Toole and his Goose," many more. Introduction and Notes by W. B. Yeats. 352pp. 5⅜ x 8½. 26941-8 Pa. $8.95

BUDDHIST MAHAYANA TEXTS, E. B. Cowell and Others (eds.). Superb, accurate translations of basic documents in Mahayana Buddhism, highly important in history of religions. The Buddha-karita of Asvaghosha, Larger Sukhavativyuha, more. 448pp. 5⅜ x 8½. 25552-2 Pa. $12.95

ONE TWO THREE . . . INFINITY: Facts and Speculations of Science, George Gamow. Great physicist's fascinating, readable overview of contemporary science: number theory, relativity, fourth dimension, entropy, genes, atomic structure, much more. 128 illustrations. Index. 352pp. 5⅜ x 8½. 25664-2 Pa. $8.95

ENGINEERING IN HISTORY, Richard Shelton Kirby, et al. Broad, nontechnical survey of history's major technological advances: birth of Greek science, industrial revolution, electricity and applied science, 20th-century automation, much more. 181 illustrations. ". . . excellent . . ."–*Isis.* Bibliography. vii + 530pp. 5⅜ x 8¼. 26412-2 Pa. $14.95

DALÍ ON MODERN ART: The Cuckolds of Antiquated Modern Art, Salvador Dalí. Influential painter skewers modern art and its practitioners. Outrageous evaluations of Picasso, Cézanne, Turner, more. 15 renderings of paintings discussed. 44 calligraphic decorations by Dalí. 96pp. 5⅜ x 8½. (USO) 29220-7 Pa. $4.95

ANTIQUE PLAYING CARDS: A Pictorial History, Henry René D'Allemagne. Over 900 elaborate, decorative images from rare playing cards (14th–20th centuries): Bacchus, death, dancing dogs, hunting scenes, royal coats of arms, players cheating, much more. 96pp. 9¼ x 12¼. 29265-7 Pa. $11.95

MAKING FURNITURE MASTERPIECES: 30 Projects with Measured Drawings, Franklin H. Gottshall. Step-by-step instructions, illustrations for constructing handsome, useful pieces, among them a Sheraton desk, Chippendale chair, Spanish desk, Queen Anne table and a William and Mary dressing mirror. 224pp. 8⅛ x 11¼. 29338-6 Pa. $13.95

THE FOSSIL BOOK: A Record of Prehistoric Life, Patricia V. Rich et al. Profusely illustrated definitive guide covers everything from single-celled organisms and dinosaurs to birds and mammals and the interplay between climate and man. Over 1,500 illustrations. 760pp. 7½ x 10⅛. 29371-8 Pa. $29.95

Prices subject to change without notice.

Available at your book dealer or write for free catalog to Dept. GI, Dover Publications, Inc., 31 East 2nd St., Mineola, N.Y. 11501. Dover publishes more than 500 books each year on science, elementary and advanced mathematics, biology, music, art, literary history, social sciences and other areas.